BRUSCHETTA

CROSTONI AND CROSTINI

BRUSCHETTA

CROSTONI AND CROSTINI

OVER 100 COUNTRY RECIPES
FROM ITALY

Ann and Franco Taruschio

PAVILION

First published in Great Britain in 1995 by
PAVILION BOOKS LIMITED
26 Upper Ground, London SE1 9PD

Text copyright © 1994 Ann and Franco Taruschio
Photographs copyright © 1994 Gus Filgate
Designed by Bernard Higton

This book is typeset in Monotype Bodoni Book

A CIP catalogue record for this book is available from the
British Library

ISBN 1 85793 474 1

Printed and bound in Spain by Cayfosa

2 4 6 8 10 9 7 5 3 1

This book may be ordered by post direct from the publisher.
Please contact the Marketing Department.
But try your bookshop first.

CONTENTS

Foreword

The recipes in this book range from the traditional to more modern and inventive. All are easy to prepare. Here in these recipes you will find a wealth of ideas which are meant to be guidelines – the cook can use his or her personal interpretation, adding this or leaving out that, adding a little more or a little less, experimenting, indulging whims. The possibilities for appetizing combinations are infinite.

Bruschetta, crostoni and crostini are so quick and easy to prepare, but please always remember to use only the best-quality extra virgin olive oil and good bread. If you do not have time to bake your own bread, buy a good firm loaf. Many supermarkets sell pain de campagne, and even ciabatta could be substituted, but never use a loaf which, when you squeeze the crumbs between your fingers, becomes a ball of dough. The bread should spring back after being squeezed. If you prefer to use brown bread instead of white bread do not worry – this is permitted. In the province of Foggia in Puglia, Southern Italy, they make bruschetta from wholemeal bread; it is known as 'cruschill'.

If you are making polenta, make extra to your requirements because slices of it can be toasted on a griddle and used instead of bread. If friends arrive unexpectedly and there is no bread in the house don't despair. Piadina or crescente can be made quickly and used as the base, following the recipes given here or adapting some of the other toppings.

Here we have food that can easily be prepared by the home cook and students who want to prepare something different but which is not too time consuming. Imagine coming back from a day's outing at the beach or in the mountains, tired but hungry. A simple, tasty bruschetta can be prepared in no time at all.

The more simple types of bruschetta – for example fettunta or the basic bruschetta of garlic and extra virgin olive oil – can be an accompaniment to a plate of mixed salumeria, prosciutto or bresaola. On the other hand, more substantial bruschette can be prepared for a light meal with friends, served with a salad and some fresh fruit to follow. What could be more pleasurable on a summer's evening?

Some recipes in this book are quite sophisticated, the peasant roots left far behind. Basically, though, brushcetta, crostoni and crostini are simple versatile dishes to be eaten as a snack, an antipasto or a light meal. They are meant to be enjoyed with *allegria*, with wine and conversation.

Traditionally, bruschetta was cooked over charcoal; today it is more often toasted on a ridged cast iron griddle. These methods give the bread a slightly charred flavour as well as an attractive ridged pattern. Crostoni are either toasted under the grill [US broiler] or in the oven, or fried in olive oil or butter. Crostini are cooked in the same way.

This is not a hard and fast rule for crostoni and crostini – they can be cooked as for bruschetta, as we have done in many of the recipes. But bruschetta would never be given the crostoni or crostini methods.

If a recipe says to grill [broil] do not be tempted to griddle because the strong charred flavour would not be suitable.

Introduction

Bruschetta originated in the central band of Italy, but has now spread to other parts. In the regions of Umbria, Tuscany, Lazio, Marche and the Abruzzi the original basic bruschetta was always the same – ½ inch slice of home-made bread, at least 2 days old, an unsalted close type of bread with a good crust, was toasted on a grill over a wood fire, rubbed with garlic while still hot and then seasoned with sea salt and extra virgin olive oil, or the first pressing before filtration of the oil. (Until not so long ago it was the custom when buying olive oil directly from the maker that he would give the customer bruschetta to taste the quality of the oil.)

Bruschetta, crostoni and crostini evolved from this original basic recipe to their present-day forms where the imagination of the cook is given free reign. Bruschetta takes its name from the fact that the slices of bread are *bruscate*, a dialect word meaning *abbrustolite*, or toasted. In Tuscany the word *fettunta*, used by the Florentines, is adopted. Fettunta literally means oiled slice. In the Lazio region they use the word *panunto* or bread with oil.

Putting food on bread certainly stems from medieval times. During that period each diner was given a thick piece of dry bread which acted as a kind of absorbent plate. This *tagliere* (or trencher), as it was called, would be given to the poor at the end of the meal. In the recipe for peposo we see an example of a very early type of bruschetta. The brickmakers cooked shin of beef in the brick kilns and then spooned it on to thick slices of toasted bread.

For the poor people of Italy bruschetta in its simplest form was often the only form of sustenance. We read in Carlo Levi's book *Christ Stopped at Eboli*, 'As for the poor they ate plain bread the whole year round, spiced occasionally with a carefully crushed raw tomato, or a little garlic and oil – or a Spanish pepper with such a devilish bite to it that it is known as a "diavolesco".'

Until the late 1950s bruschette or crostini were eaten for *merenda* (snack) by school children and *contadini* (farmers). The *vagara* (housewife) would bring the slices of toasted bread wrapped in a blue and white checked *sparra* or *stroffinaccio* (cloth), along with a salami, some olives, a bottle of olive oil, some garlic and a terracotta flask of wine drawn straight from the barrel. All these would be placed inside a basket. The *vagara* would balance the basket on her head and walk to the field straight backed, hips swinging, where the farm workers would be sitting under a shady tree for their morning rest, having been hard at work since the early hours. The bruschetta would be handed round, garlic rubbed on, olive oil dribbled over, some salami roughly sliced on top or a slice or two of prosciutto and a few black olives added and *via* – the *merenda* was ready to be washed down with the cool fresh white wine. As working the land has become mechanized so the custom of taking *merenda* to the fields has become less and less common.

In the Veneto and Lombardy it was the custom to season the toasted bread with a pesto of bacon fat mixed with a little garlic and parsley. Once these primitive bruschetta were eaten to fill the eater up, to quell his hunger. Huge slices of bread were used, but now the slices are smaller and toppings of every kind can be used. We eat bruschetta now not so much to quell our hunger as to stimulate our taste buds. As for the children in the

1990's they prefer the fast food or sweet preparations for their *merenda*!

The following recipes are a mixture of old and new, culled from various sources, but primarily from a group of ladies at Porto Recanati near Ancona on the Adriatic coast of Italy. I was there with my teenage daughter. Trying to make myself scarce whilst the handsome young Romeos pursued my daughter, I decided to research recipes for this book, still keeping a hopefully discreet watchful eye. The ladies sitting near me on the beach became curious and wanted to know what this English woman was up to. I explained that I was researching for a book on bruschetta. Every day from then on there would almost be a competition to see who could bring me the most recipes – not just recipes for bruschetta but also their particular regional recipes. There was a gynaecologist from Cremona, and the direttrice of a bank who was originally from Sardinia but for the past 20 years had been living in the Abruzzi, and so on, all professional ladies from different regions of Italy. During my 10 days spent on the beach, I rarely heard these ladies talk about their respective jobs – it was always about food and their families.

The ladies spent a month of *riposo* (rest) on the beach every year, some with their children or grandchildren. Their husbands visited them at the weekends. I was very touched the weekend that I was there to discover that husbands had been commissioned to bring bunches of fresh peppers, a special cheese, and more recipes. I must also add that even some of the young Romeos eventually brought recipes collected from grandmothers and mothers.

Further to our researches on the beach, we also toured the regions of Emilia – Romagna, the Marche, Umbria, the Abruzzi and Molise in search of recipes. All have been tested and nearly all have appeared at some time or another on the menu of our restaurant, the Walnut Tree Inn, near Abergavenny in Wales, run by my Italian husband Franco and myself.

Making the Four Essential Breads

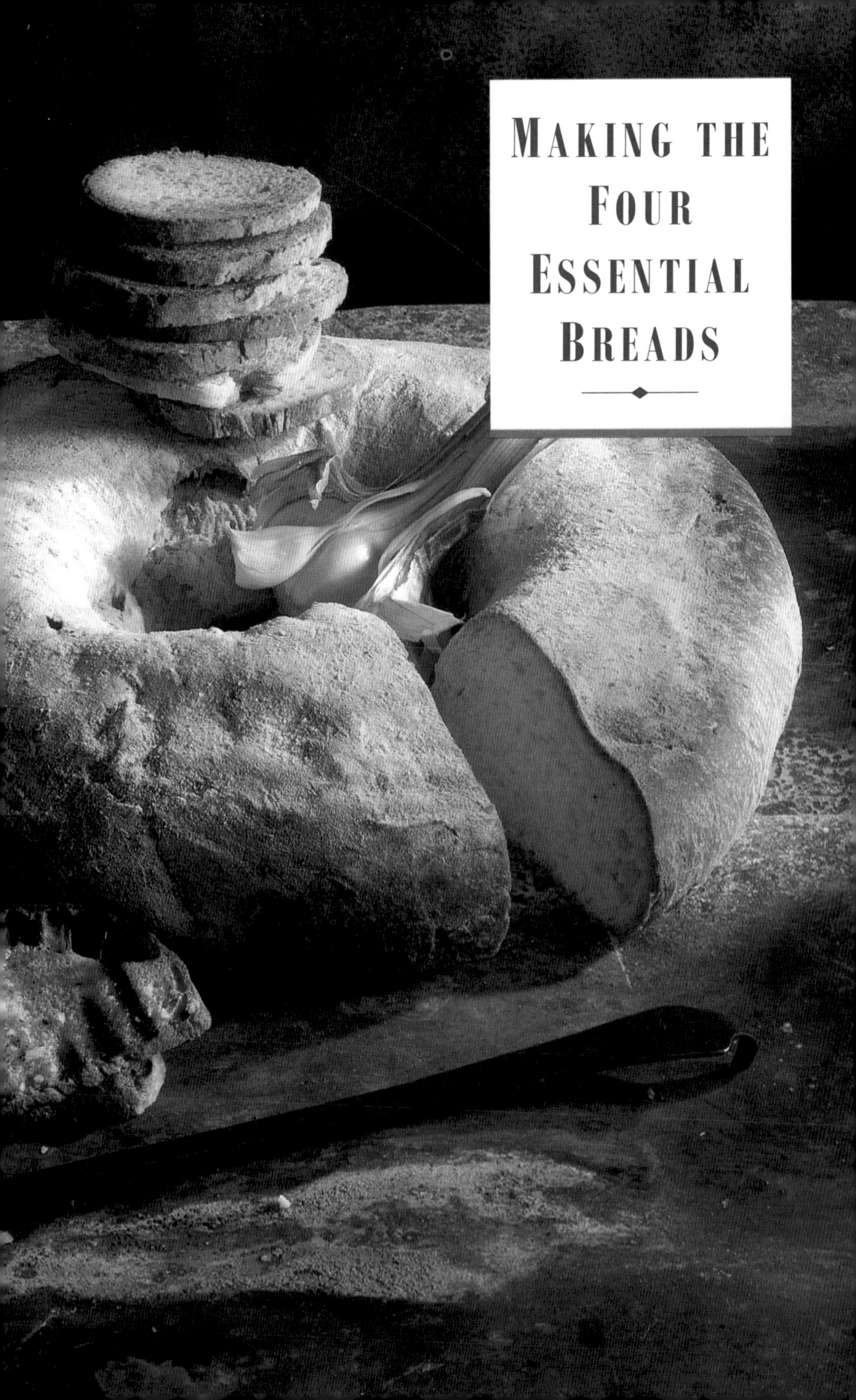

Bread – the staff of life

All through the ages bread has been a fundamental part of mankind's existence. For many ancient cultures bread symbolized immortality, fertility and rebirth. In Egypt bread was offered up to Iside, the harvest goddess. In Arabic, the same word is used to define bread and life. In Italy bread represents providence, grace and the Eucharist. For both Christians and Jews bread has a special symbolism. The Christians say in the Lord's Prayer, 'Give us this day our daily bread', and in the Eucharist unleavened bread represents the body of Christ. The Jews recall their flight from Egypt with unleavened bread.

According to legend, when the Jews fled Egypt 3000 years ago they left in such haste that the bread they baked to eat on their journey was not given time to rise. To commemorate this event, Jews eat matzo, unleavened bread, during Passover. For the Seder, the central event of Passover, three matzos are placed under a cloth in the centre of the Seder table, to become the focus of the evening's activities. The three matzos represent the three sects of Israel: the Cohamin, who were the highest religious authority, the Levites, who administered and served the Temples' needs, and the Israelites . . . the people.

In the Old Testament there is considerable mention of

unleavened bread. For example, in Genesis 19.3 it is written that Lot 'made them a feast and baked unleavened bread and they ate'.

Bread in one form or another is one of the oldest foods in the world. Its ancestry can be traced back to Neolithic times, when a flat type of bread, probably made from barley, was cooked on red hot stones on an open fire. The Neolithic cook discovered that grain left to sprout became more digestible, and then learned that the dried sprouted grain could be pounded and used to make bread.

Pestles and mortars and primitive milling equipment found during excavations in the Nile valley are proof that the ancient Egyptians ground grain to make flour for bread. We know from residues of grain found in these pieces of equipment that barley and a type of wheat, a precursor to the type grown nowadays, were used. The remains of bread ovens were also found, believed to be the first ever constructed.

Rye and oats were known and used for bread during the Bronze Age. Millet is another bread-making grain first used in Neolithic times. It is still made into bread by the people of North African countries.

The use of yeast in bread making came later, approximately 6000 years ago. The Sumerians, who lived in the fertile valleys of Mesopotamia, understood the use of yeast for making beer and a light form of bread. It was the Egyptians, however, who perfected the use of yeast and who made the art of bread-making a profession. It is said that an Egyptian baker left some dough out in the warm sun and it fermented, thus producing the first sour dough.

The first primitive breads were round flat discs cooked on a bake stone, like the piada or piadina of Emiglia Romagna. In ancient times piadina were made from an unleavened mixture of flour and water, a very basic pancake cooked on hot stones. This bread is still cooked on a scorching hot clay disc and heated on an open wood fire, although a flat griddle is more often used on top of a stove. Over the years lard, olive oil or butter and also salt have been added to the original mixture. When cooked and still hot the piadina has either prosciutto, sausage, bacon or a soft cheese put on top and it is folded over to facilitate eating by hand. Poets have composed poems in honour of the piadina, and historians write about its past. To the Romagnoli the piadina is part of the soul of Romagna. The Piadina is the precursor of the pizza.

The bread made in Puglia is particularly suitable for bruschetta. I have given two recipes, one slightly more complicated than the other but neither to be afraid of. The Pugliese bread is a large crusty loaf weighing 1–2 kilos, which originated from a bread brought by the Turkish conquerors who baked their chewy porous bread in wood burning stoves. Pane pugliese is a real rustic type of bread meant to be cut in thick slices. Tradition has it that the bread is normally held against the chest and sliced towards the body with a sharp knife, a practice best left to the Pugliese! A Pugliese legend says that one who wastes even crumbs of this loaf will be condemned to Purgatory for as many years as there are crumbs.

Bread in Italy is never wasted – it is considered sacrilegious to throw it away. If bread is dropped and where it fell is not too dirty, it is first kissed and then used. If the bread is dirty it is given to the animals but never discarded. Bruschetta is one way of using up bread which is past its best but not stale. Theresa, who comes from Puglia and who taught us how to make the first pane pugliese recipe, always makes the sign of the cross over the bread before leaving it to rise. Reverence is shown to bread, even to this day, in many parts of Italy.

PANE PUGLIESE

(TERESA'S)

Teresa is a farmer's wife from Albarella in
Puglia who when visiting her son in Wales came to cook
with us for a day. Her recipe is completely unorthodox
but it works.

MAKES 1 BIG LOAF

*1 kg/2 lb 3 oz strong white flour [US 7 cups white
bread flour]*

*10 g/¼ oz fresh yeast [US ½ package
compressed yeast]*

*12 g/scant ½ oz sea salt [US 1½ tablespoons
coarse salt]*

½ litre/16 fl oz warm water

150 ml/¼ pt water at room temperature [US ⅔ cup]

Put the flour on a working table and make a well in the
centre. Crumble the yeast round the edge of the well and
add the salt. Pour the warm water into the well. Gently
add the flour to the well, amalgamating the flour and
water as you go. Knead for about 5 minutes to a very firm
dough.

Now sprinkle some of the room temperature water on
top of the dough and knead until amalgamated. Keep on
doing this process of sprinkling water and kneading until
all the water is used up. The dough will seem very strange
and the texture will be very sloppy when you add the
second amount of water. But do not worry – just keep
kneading until all the water is absorbed before sprinkling
on the next lot of water. Lightly dust the work surface
with flour, give the dough one final knead and then place
it in a large mixing bowl. Cover the surface of the dough
with a lightly oiled piece of film and place a cloth on top
to cover. Leave the dough to rise in a warm place for 1½
hours.

Remove the dough from the bowl and knead again
briefly. Shape the dough into a large round, flat loaf,

place it on a baking tray and leave, covered with a cloth, to rise for 1 hour in a warm place.

Bake in an oven preheated to 180°C/350°F/gas 4 for 35 minutes. Turn the loaf over after 15 minutes baking. Leave the loaf to cool on a rack.

PANE PUGLIESE

This is the more conventional recipe

MAKES 2 BIG LOAVES

2 kg/4½ lb strong white flour [US 14 cups white bread flour]

40 g/1½ oz fresh yeast [US 2 packages compressed yeast]

1.6 litres/just under 3 pints [US 6¾ cups] tepid water

10 g/¼ oz [US 1 tablespoon] liquid malt extract

40 g/1½ oz sea salt [US 4½ tablespoons coarse salt]

Dissolve the yeast in a little tepid water. Mix all the ingredients together and knead for 20 minutes. Cover the dough and leave it to rise for 2 hours in a warm place.

Knead the dough lightly, then divide it into two and leave it to rise again with the folding side of the dough – as opposed to the smooth side – face up. After 30 minutes flatten the round shape of dough, turn it over and leave to rise for another 30 minutes. Bake the loaves in an oven preheated to 220°C/425°F/gas 7 for 20–30 minutes, then reduce the oven to 180°C/350°F/gas 4 and bake for a final 10 minutes.

Do not open the oven door during the first 30 minutes of baking because it can ruin the bread if the temperature drops. It is advisable to place a container full of water in the oven to create a slightly humid atmosphere. The baked bread should have a dry hollow sound when the base is tapped with the knuckles.

PANE FILONE

Filone are perfect for crostini. A French baguette can be
used as a substitute.

MAKES 2 LOAVES

First dough

60 g/2 oz fresh yeast [US 3 packages compressed yeast]

170 ml/6 fl oz [US ¾ cup] lukewarm water

*220 g/7¾ oz strong white flour [US 2 cups white
bread flour]*

Second dough

340 ml/12 fl oz [US 1½ cups] lukewarm water

1 pinch salt

*550 g/1¼ lb strong white flour [US 5 cups white
bread flour]*

To make the first dough, dissolve the yeast in the water.
Put the flour in a large bowl and make a well in it. Pour
the dissolved yeast into the well and mix with a wooden
spoon, adding the flour to make a thick batter. Cover the
bowl with a towel and leave overnight in a warm draught-
free place.

The following day, continue with the second dough: add
the water a little at a time to the batter, stirring contin-
uously with a wooden spoon to dissolve it. Add the salt
and then four-fifths of the flour a little at a time, while
stirring with a wooden spoon. Cover the bowl with a cloth
and leave the dough to rest for ½ an hour.

Spread out the remaining flour on a work top and put
the risen dough on it. Knead the dough, working in the
rest of the flour. Divide the dough in half and shape each
piece into a filone – long rolled loaf 6 cm/2½ in wide.
Wrap each loaf in a cloth and leave to rest for 15 minutes.

Unwrap the loaves and place on a preheated baking tile.
Bake for about 1 hour in an oven preheated to 200°C/
400°F/gas 6.

CRESCENTE

Farina 'O' is Italian flour and is available in most continental delicatessens or speciality food stores.

MAKES 18

Crescente are served with prosciutto, salami or a fresh (not matured) cheese. This dough does not have to be used all at once as it will keep for 2 days.

500 g/1¼ lb type 'O' flour [US 3½ cups type 'O' flour]

1 teaspoon salt

1 good pinch bicarbonate of soda [US baking soda]

300 ml/½ pt [US 1¼ cups] milk, approximately

extra virgin olive oil

sea salt

Knead the flour, salt, bicarbonate of soda and milk together to make a dough. Wrap the dough in a cloth and leave to rest in the refrigerator for 1 hour.

Break off pieces of dough the size of a golf ball and roll out into discs about 18 cm/7 in diameter.

Heat a little extra virgin olive oil in a heavy non-stick frying pan. Fry the discs, one at a time, until golden on both sides; they will bubble all over. Change the olive oil in the pan every 2 or 3 discs. Drain on kitchen paper, sprinkle with freshly ground sea salt and serve at once.

Ammazafame
This literally translates as 'kill the hunger'. When bread is being made, small pieces of dough can be rolled out the size of a crêpe and then fried in olive oil. Sprinkled with a little sea salt and eaten while still hot with a slice of prosciutto, they certainly 'kill the hunger'!

PIADINA

A testo is a disc of fireproof clay (terracotta). Never be tempted to oil either the clay disc or the cast iron griddle when making piadina.
A welsh griddle – the type used for making welsh cakes – can be used failing a testo, or a very heavy frying pan if desperate!
Piadina can be frozen and rewarmed by wrapping them when defrosted in foil and leaving in a hot oven until reheated.

MAKES 4–6

500 g/1¼ lb plain flour [US 3½ cups all-purpose flour]

30 g/1 oz [US 2 tablespoons] butter

salt

tepid water

Put the flour in a mound on a working table. Add the butter, slightly melted, and some lightly salted tepid water, sufficient to make a dough. Knead thoroughly for 10 minutes, then wrap the dough in a cloth and place under an inverted bowl. Leave to rest for 30 minutes.

Break off pieces of the dough the size of a mandarin orange. Roll out into discs not thicker than 5 mm/¼ in.

Heat a testo or flat cast iron griddle either on a wood fire or on the top of a stove. When the griddle is hot place a disc of dough on it and leave to cook for a few minutes. When the base seems cooked turn the piadina over and cook for a further few minutes. The piadina will have developed slightly burned bubbles which give off a wonderful appetizing smell of bread.

As the piadina are made keep them warm in a cloth folded a few times. Piadina are best served hot.

———◆———

POLENTA FOR BRUSCHETTA, CROSTONI AND CROSTINI

SERVES 4

300 g / 10 oz [US 1⅔ cups] polenta flour
a bare litre / 1⅔ pints [US just under 1 quart] water
1 pinch of salt

Bring the water to the boil and add a pinch of salt. Add the polenta flour to the boiling water (the water must be boiling because a high temperature is needed to burst the starch grains), letting it fall in like sand sifting through your fingers. As the flour is falling into the water, stir with a wooden spoon. Always stir in one direction; never change direction. Keep stirring for 30 – 40 minutes. You should end up with quite a thick paste, but not too thick to pour.

Pour the polenta about 1 cm / ½ in thick on to a lightly oiled shallow pan. A swiss roll tin [US jelly roll pan] would be fine. Leave to get cold and then cut into rectangles or squares for bruschetta, crostoni or crostini.

Alternatively, pour the polenta into a lightly oiled round-bottomed bowl. When cold, turn out the polenta and slice as normal for bruschetta, crostoni or crostini. Polenta is easier to cut the traditional way with a taut strong thread.

THE RECIPES

VEGETABLE BRUSCHETTA

BRUSCHETTA CON POMODORI VERDI MARINATI

BRUSCHETTA WITH MARINATED GREEN TOMATOES

This recipe is from Edda Servi Machlin's book,
The Classic Cuisine of the Italian Jews.

MAKES APPROX. 1.2 LITRES / 2 PT [US 5 CUPS] OF
MARINATED GREEN TOMATOES

1.4 kg / 3 lb green tomatoes

coarse sea salt

white wine vinegar

3 large cloves garlic, finely chopped

2 tablespoons fennel seeds

2 tablespoons dried oregano

2 tablespoons balsamic vinegar

6 small hot chilli peppers

extra virgin olive oil

Wash the tomatoes but don't dry them. Slice them thinly, collecting all the juice in a bowl as you slice. Arrange the sliced tomatoes in the bowl in layers, sprinkling each layer with coarse sea salt. Place a large plate or bowl directly on top of the tomatoes and put a weight on the plate. Leave the tomatoes to marinate for 5 hours.

Drain thoroughly. Add white wine vinegar to cover the tomatoes and leave for another 4 hours, then drain again.

Layer the tomatoes into a sterilized jar, sprinkling each layer with small amounts of garlic, fennel seeds and oregano and a few drops of balsamic vinegar. Distribute the chilli peppers here and there throughout the jar. Pour extra virgin olive oil over the tomatoes, shaking the jar to remove any air pockets. Cover tightly and store in a cool place. These tomatoes can be eaten after 5 days but will last for 5 months.

Serve on bruschetta.

Previous pages:
Bruschetta with Grilled Vegetables (page 51)

PANUNTO O FETTUNTA

Fettunta is the dialect word in Tuscany for bruschetta

SERVES 4

4 slices of bread for bruschetta
2 cloves garlic, very finely chopped
extra virgin olive oil
4 plum tomatoes, peeled, seeded and diced
salt and freshly ground black pepper

Toast the bread on a griddle. Spread the garlic over the slices, sprinkle with olive oil, spoon over the tomato dice and season with salt and pepper. Serve.

◆

BRUSCHETTA TRICOLORI

THREE-COLOURED BRUSCHETTA

SERVES 4

4 slices of bread for bruschetta
4 ripe plum tomatoes
1 medium onion
24 thin slices of cucumber
dried oregano
salt and freshly ground black pepper
extra virgin olive oil

Slice the tomatoes and onions thinly. Toast the bread on a griddle. Layer the tomatoes and cucumber on the top, then scatter the rings of onion over the tomato and cucumber. Sprinkle dried oregano over, season with salt and freshly ground black pepper and dress with a little extra virgin olive oil. Serve.

BRUSCHETTA SAPORITA

PIQUANT BRUSCHETTA

SERVES 4

4 slices of bread for bruschetta
4 tomatoes, peeled, seeded and finely diced
8 anchovy fillets, 4 of them finely chopped
12 salted capers, rinsed, dried and roughly chopped
2 cloves garlic, finely chopped
3 fresh basil leaves, torn into small pieces
1 good pinch dried oregano
freshly ground black pepper
salt if necessary
2 tablespoons extra virgin olive oil

Place the diced tomato in a bowl and add the finely chopped anchovies and the capers. Add the garlic, basil and oregano. Season with pepper and with salt if necessary (the salt in the anchovies might be sufficient). Stir in the extra virgin olive oil.

Toast the bread on a griddle and spread the tomato mixture on top. Decorate each bruschetta with an anchovy fillet. Serve at once.

◆

BRUSCHETTA DI POMODORI MAJORCA

BRUSCHETTA WITH TOMATOES MAJORCAN-STYLE

Home-made vinegar is especially good for this dish.

SERVES 4

4 slices of bread for bruschetta
1 clove garlic
4 plum tomatoes
extra virgin olive oil
salt

red wine vinegar
24 Niçoise olives, pitted and coarsely chopped
6 teaspoons salted capers, rinsed and dried

Toast the bread on a griddle and rub with garlic. Slice the tomatoes wafer thin and spread over the toast, pressing them down lightly. Drizzle olive oil over the tomatoes to taste and season with salt. Carefully shake a few drops of red wine vinegar over the tomatoes. Scatter the olives and capers on top and serve.

BRUSCHETTA AL POMODORO

BRUSCHETTA WITH TOMATOES

SERVES 4

4 slices of bread for bruschetta
6 plum tomatoes
6 fresh basil leaves, torn into pieces
1 clove garlic, finely chopped
salt and freshly ground black pepper
8 black olives, pitted and roughly chopped
extra virgin olive oil

Peel and seed the tomatoes and cut into small cubes. Season with the basil, garlic, salt and freshly ground black pepper. Add the olives to the tomatoes. Barely cover the mixture with extra virgin olive oil and stir well in. Leave for 20 minutes before using.

Toast the slices of bread on a griddle. Divide the tomato mixture among the bruschetta and serve at once.

Previous pages:
Bruschetta with Marinated Green Tomatoes (page 26)
Bruschetta with Tomatoes (page 31)

BRUSCHETTA CON POMODORI E RUCOLA

BRUSCHETTA WITH TOMATOES AND ROCKET

This is a recipe from Puglia.

SERVES 6

6 slices of bread for bruschetta
450 g / 1 lb plum tomatoes
115 g / 4 oz rocket [US arugula]
6 tablespoons extra virgin olive oil
salt and freshly ground black pepper
garlic (optional)

Peel the tomatoes by making a slight prick in the skin and briefly dropping them into boiling water. Refresh the tomatoes under cold water; the skin will come off easily. Seed the tomatoes and cut them into small cubes.

Remove the stalks of the rocket, thoroughly wash and dry. Lightly dress the rocket leaves with some of the olive oil and season with salt and pepper. Toss well to make sure each leaf has a thin film of oil.

Toast the bread on a griddle and rub with garlic, if you like. Drizzle the rest of the oil on the toast. Distribute the tomato cubes between the bruschetta, season lightly with salt and put the dressed rocket on top. Serve.

◆

BRUSCHETTA DI LUNGA VITA

BRUSCHETTA 'LONG LIFE'

SERVES 4

4 slices of bread for bruschetta
4 tomatoes, peeled, seeded and cut into small cubes
1 small hot chilli pepper, finely chopped
1 tablespoon fennel seeds
2 tablespoons extra virgin olive oil
salt and freshly ground black pepper
1 clove garlic

Mix the tomatoes, chilli, fennel seeds, extra virgin olive oil, salt and freshly ground black pepper. Leave to marinate for 2 hours.

Toast the bread on a griddle, rub with garlic and spoon the tomato mixture on top. Serve.

CROSTONI AGLI ASPARAGI E FONTINA

CROSTONI WITH ASPARAGUS AND FONTINA

SERVES 4

4 slices of bread for crostoni

500 g / 1¼ lb asparagus

4 slices of fontina cheese, total weight 100 g / 3½ oz

50 g / 1¾ oz [US 3½ tablespoons] butter

lemon

salt and freshly ground black pepper

shavings of Parmesan cheese

Wash the asparagus thoroughly. Trim the stalks, removing the tough part. Bring a large pan of salted water to the boil and cook the asparagus for 15 minutes, or steam them, until a fork easily pierces the thick part of the stalk. Drain the asparagus and keep them warm.

Toast the bread on a griddle and butter them with some of the butter. Divide the asparagus among the toast. Dribble a little more melted butter on top of the asparagus and cover with a slice of fontina. Place the crostoni under a hot grill [US broiler] to melt the cheese.

Lightly poach the eggs in water seasoned with lemon juice and salt. Place a poached egg on top of each crostoni, dribble the rest of the melted butter over each egg and season with freshly ground black pepper. Shave Parmesan on top. Serve at once.

Overleaf:

Crostini with Asparagus and Prosciutto (page 36)

Crostoni with Asparagus and Fontina (page 33)

Three-Coloured Bruschetta (page 27)

CROSTINI DI ASPARAGI AL PROSCIUTTO

CROSTINI WITH ASPARAGUS AND PROSCIUTTO

SERVES 4

12 slices of bread for crostini

1½ kg/3½ lb asparagus

12 slices of Parma ham

115 g/4 oz [US ½ cup] butter (more may be needed)

*4 tablespoons freshly grated Parmesan cheese
(more may be needed)*

salt

Trim the asparagus, leaving 8 cm/3 in of the stalk. (The remaining part of the stalks can be used for soup.) Cook the asparagus in lightly salted water until just al dente. Drain.

Melt the butter and dip the asparagus in it, then roll each asparagus in freshly grated Parmesan cheese. Divide the asparagus into 12 bundles and wrap a slice of Parma ham round each bundle.

Butter a gratin dish which will hold the bundles in one layer. Sprinkle over any remaining Parmesan cheese and any butter left from dipping the asparagus. If none was left over, use some more. Place the gratin dish in an oven preheated to 180°C/350°F/gas 4 and cook for 10 minutes.

While the asparagus are in the oven, fry the slices of bread in butter. Serve each asparagus bundle on a crostini and eat at once.

◆

CROSTONI DEL GHIOTTONE

CROSTONI GOURMAND

SERVES 4

4 slices of bread for crostoni

extra virgin olive oil

1 spring onion [US scallion], finely chopped

65 g / 2¾ oz mushrooms preserved in oil
4 salted anchovies, rinsed and dried
1 teaspoon dried oregano
1 tablespoon finely chopped parsley
salt and freshly ground black pepper
200 ml / 7 fl oz [US ⅞ cup] béchamel sauce (see below)

Toast the bread on a griddle, then sprinkle with olive oil and the finely chopped spring onion. Divide the mushrooms among the crostoni. Place an anchovy on top of each and sprinkle with oregano and parsley. Season with salt and freshly ground black pepper. Cover each crostoni with béchamel.

Bake in an oven preheated to 200°C/400°F/gas 6 for 10 minutes. Serve at once.

BÉCHAMEL SAUCE

MAKES 750 ML / 1¼ PT [US 3 CUPS]

600 ml / 1 pt [US 2½ cups] milk
1 small onion
1 bay leaf
2 sprigs parsley
1 clove
1 blade mace
salt
6 peppercorns
60 g / 2 oz [US 4 tablespoons] butter
60 g / 2 oz plain flour [US 4 tablespoons all-purpose flour]

Warm the milk with the onion, herbs, spices, salt and peppercorns, bringing it slowly to simmering point. Cover the pan and leave to infuse off the heat for half an hour. Strain the milk.

Melt the butter in a saucepan, add the flour and mix in

well making a roux. Cook the roux for a few minutes, taking care not to let it colour. Slowly add the milk beating it in with a balloon whisk. Bring the sauce to the boil, whisking constantly. The sauce should be smooth. Check the seasoning before using.

CROSTINI AI FUNGHI PORCINI

CROSTINI OF PORCINI

SERVES 6

12 slices of bread for crostini

800 g / 1¾ lb fresh porcini (ceps) or cultivated mushrooms

15 g / ½ oz dried sliced porcini if using cultivated mushrooms

1 clove garlic, finely chopped

3 tablespoons extra virgin olive oil

flour

170 ml / 6 fl oz [US ¾ cup] milk warmed

3 tablespoons finely chopped parsley

40 g / 1½ oz [US ⅓ cup] freshly grated Parmesan cheese

salt and freshly ground black pepper

If using dried mushrooms soak them for half an hour. Slice the fresh mushrooms and fry them with the dried ones and the garlic in olive oil. Dust lightly with flour, add the warmed milk and stir in thoroughly. Add the parsley and Parmesan and season with salt and freshly ground black pepper.

Toast the bread on a griddle. Drizzle a little extra virgin olive oil on the crostini, then spoon the mushroom sauce on top. Serve at once.

CROSTINI DI FUNGHI TRIFOLATI

CROSTINI WITH FINELY CHOPPED MUSHROOMS, GARLIC
AND HERBS

The mushroom mixture is also good served on
bruschetta rubbed with garlic and which have been
dribbled with olive oil.

MAKES 50 CROSTINI

50 slices of bread for crostini

*1.4 kg/3 lb field mushrooms, or cultivated ones, roughly
chopped*

115 g/4 oz [US ½ cup] butter

2 large onions, finely chopped

4 cloves garlic, finely chopped

150 ml/¼ pt [US ⅔ cup] dry white wine

salt and freshly ground black pepper

2 heaped tablespoons chopped parsley

½ teaspoon chopped thyme

nutmeg

Melt the butter and fry the onion and garlic until golden.
Add the mushrooms and fry. Pour in the wine and season
with salt and pepper. Drain off the liquor from the
mushrooms and reduce to a thick syrupy texture. Pass the
mushrooms through a food processor until chopped
finely, like grains, then return the mushrooms to the
liquor. Add the parsley, thyme and nutmeg. Check the
seasoning. This mixture should be firm, not sloppy.

Lightly butter the slices of bread and toast in a medium
oven until pale gold. Serve the mushroom mixture on the
crostini.

◆

CROSTINI ALLE OLIVE E FUNGHI

CROSTINI WITH OLIVES AND MUSHROOMS

SERVES 6

6 slices of bread for crostini
60 g / 2 oz pitted black olives
315 g / 10 oz button mushrooms
4 tablespoons extra virgin olive oil
1 clove garlic, finely chopped
salt and freshly ground black pepper

Slice the mushrooms. Heat half the olive oil in a frying pan, add the mushrooms and garlic and fry for 3–4 minutes or until just tender. Season with salt and freshly ground black pepper.

Toast the crostini on a griddle.

Combine the olives and the remaining olive oil in a food processor and purée. Spread the olive paste on the toast and cover with the mushrooms. Serve at once.

◆

CROSTINI AI FUNGHI

CROSTINI WITH MUSHROOMS

SERVES 4

4 slices of bread for crostini
250 g / 9 oz cultivated mushrooms, thinly sliced
1 small onion, finely chopped
1 clove garlic, finely chopped
extra virgin olive oil
salt and freshly ground black pepper
1 tablespoon salted capers, rinsed, dried and roughly chopped
1 tablespoon finely chopped parsley

Fry the onion and garlic in olive oil until soft and golden. Add the mushrooms and fry. Season with salt and freshly ground black pepper. Add the chopped capers.

Toast the bread on a griddle and put the mushroom mixture on top. Sprinkle with parsley and serve at once.

◆

BRUSCHETTA CON PORCINI TRIFOLATI

BRUSCHETTA WITH PORCINI MUSHROOMS IN GARLIC
AND PARSLEY

SERVES 4

4 slices of bread for bruschetta

450 g / 1 lb fresh porcini (ceps)

15 g / ½ oz [US 1 tablespoon] butter

4 tablespoons extra virgin olive oil

1 bunch of parsley, finely chopped

1 clove garlic, finely chopped

salt and freshly ground black pepper

Clean and thinly slice the porcini. Heat the butter and oil, add the parsley and garlic and fry briefly. Add the sliced porcini and fry gently until cooked. Season with salt and freshly ground black pepper.

Toast the bread on a griddle. Serve the mushrooms divided among the toasted bread. Serve at once.

LENTICCHIE E PANE FRITTO

LENTILS AND FRIED BREAD

SERVES 4

4 slices of bread for crostoni
450 g / 1 lb [US 2¼ cups] lentils
1 bay leaf
5 sprigs parsley
1 clove garlic
½ stalk celery
stock
3 tablespoons extra virgin olive oil
salt and freshly ground black pepper
2–3 eggs
450 ml / ¾ pt [US 2 cups] light olive oil for frying

Cook the lentils with the herbs, garlic and celery in enough stock to cover them well. Half way through the cooking add the 3 tablespoons of extra virgin olive oil.

Dip the crostoni in seasoned beaten egg and fry in light olive oil.

Serve the lentils on top of the crostoni.

BRUSCHETTA CON CIME DI ZUCCHINI

BRUSCHETTA WITH ZUCCHINI TOPS

When the zucchini plants have finished flowering you are left with little clusters of tiny zucchini and tender leaves sprouting from the top. Before you pull the plants up, nip these tops off: the clusters should be cut about 8–10cm/3–4 in long. It is a tradition in the Marche to serve these cime di zucchini with bruschetta as a first course or as a *contorno*, a side vegetable dish. In the early part of the autumn women from the farms bring bunches of these cime to sell in the markets. Everyone loves these final offerings of the summer season.

SERVES 4

550 g/1¼ lb zucchini tops
4 tablespoons extra virgin olive oil
2 cloves garlic, finely chopped
coarse sea salt and freshly ground black pepper
4 slices of bread or cold polenta for bruschetta
wedges of lemon

Steam the zucchini tops for about 10 minutes. Heat the olive oil in a frying pan and add the finely chopped garlic. Fry briefly, then, add the zucchini tops and fry them, being careful not to break them up. Season with coarse sea salt and freshly ground black pepper.

Toast the bread or polenta slices on a griddle. Serve the zucchini tops on the bruschetta, with a wedge of lemon.

◆

BRUSCHETTA CON MELANZANE ALLA CALABRESE

BRUSCHETTA WITH AUBERGINES CALABRESE

Good as a first course or as a vegetable with simply cooked meat

SERVES 8

8 slices of bread for bruschetta

2 aubergines [US eggplants], weighing approx. 450 g / 1 lb each

coarse salt

6 plum tomatoes or ripe ordinary tomatoes, peeled, seeded and diced

2 cloves garlic, finely chopped

2 tablespoons light olive oil

2 hot red chilli peppers, seeded and sliced thinly

1 sprig parsley, chopped

6 fresh mint leaves, chopped

freshly ground black pepper

Wash the aubergines and slice lengthwise, about 1cm/½ in thick. Sprinkle the slices with salt and leave in a colander to drain for 1 hour. Dry the slices well, then place them on a preheated ridged griddle and cook until lightly brown on either side, turning once only. Keep warm.

Fry the garlic briefly in the olive oil. Add the diced tomatoes and sauté briefly; they must keep their dice shape. Add the chilli and herbs and season with salt and pepper.

Toast the bread on a griddle. Arrange the aubergine slices on the bruschetta. Spoon the tomato mixture on top of the aubergine slices. Serve either hot or at room temperature.

CROSTONI ALLE MELANZANE IN POTACCHIO

CROSTONI WITH AUBERGINES IN POTACCHIO

In potacchio is a Marchigiani method of cooking in
wine, tomato, rosemary and garlic.

SERVES 4

4 slices of bread for crostoni

3 aubergines [US eggplants]

*150 g / 5 oz [US ¾ cup] peeled, seeded and chopped
tomatoes (concassé)*

4 tablespoons extra virgin olive oil

2 cloves garlic, 1 of them finely chopped

1 sprig of rosemary

1 glass dry white wine

salt and freshly ground black pepper

150 g / 5 oz fontina cheese

Wash and dry the aubergines and cut them into small
cubes. Sprinkle the cubes with salt, place in a colander
and leave to drain for 20 minutes. Dry the cubes.

Heat the extra virgin olive oil and fry the finely chopped
garlic with the sprig of rosemary. Add the cubes of
aubergine and fry until golden. Add the white wine and
briskly reduce, then add the tomato concassé and season
with freshly ground black pepper. Cook gently for 15
minutes, stirring regularly. Remove the rosemary from
the mixture.

Toast the bread under a grill [US broiler], then rub with
the remaining clove of garlic. Divide the aubergine mixture among the crostoni. Chop the fontina cheese into
small cubes and scatter on top of the aubergine mixture.
Put the crostoni under the hot grill until the cheese has
melted. Serve at once.

◆

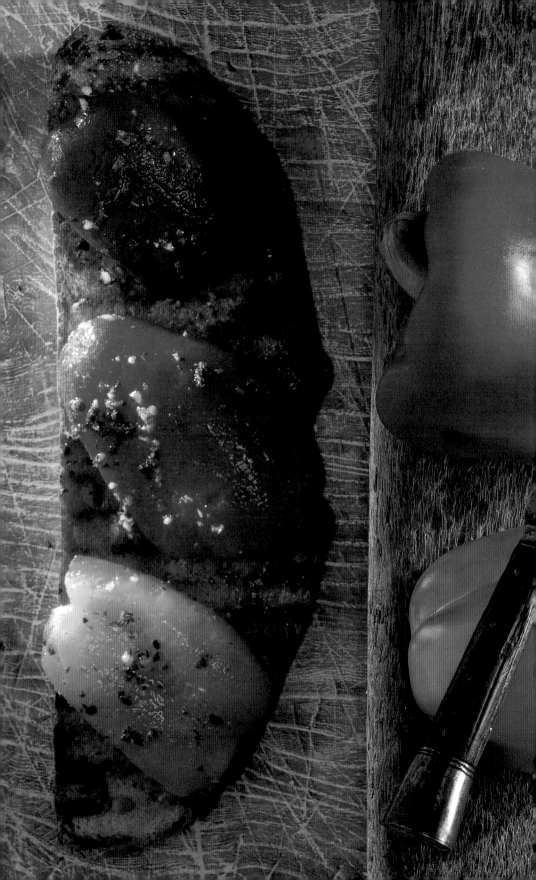

CROSTINI DI PEPERONI IMBOTTITI

CROSTINI OF STUFFED PEPPERS

SERVES 4

8 slices of bread for crostini

2 red sweet peppers

2 yellow sweet peppers

extra virgin olive oil

100 g/4 oz bread, cut in tiny dice

30 g/1 oz salted anchovies, rinsed, dried and chopped

30 g/1 oz black olives, pitted and chopped

1 teaspoon salted capers, rinsed and dried

1 clove garlic, finely chopped

1 tablespoon each chopped parsley and dried oregano

salt and freshly ground black pepper

Remove the skin of the peppers by charring with a blow torch, an invaluable utensil in the kitchen, or over a gas flame.

Cut the peppers in half and remove the seeds. Place in a baking tray and drizzle olive oil over them. Bake in an oven preheated to 160°C/300°F/gas 2 for 15 minutes.

Fry the bread cubes in hot oil, drain and put in a bowl. Add the anchovies, olives, capers, garlic, herbs, and salt and pepper to taste. Mix the ingredients together and use to fill the pepper halves. Drizzle a little of the pepper cooking juices over and return the peppers to the oven for another 10 minutes.

Toast the bread on a griddle. Serve the warm pepper halves on the crostini, 1 red and 1 yellow per person.

———◆———

Previous pages:
Bruschetta with Peppers (page 49)

BRUSCHETTA AI PEPERONI

BRUSCHETTA WITH PEPPERS

SERVES 4

4 slices of bread for bruschetta
1 large yellow sweet pepper
1 large red sweet pepper
1 large green sweet pepper
3 cloves garlic, finely chopped
2 tablespoons finely chopped parsley
salt and freshly ground black pepper
extra virgin olive oil

Skin the peppers by holding them over a high gas flame to char the skins, or use a blow torch to burn the skin off. Make sure all the skin is removed. Cut the peppers into 4 and remove the seeds and ribs. Place the peppers in a shallow dish and season with the garlic, parsley, salt, freshly ground black pepper and a liberal amount of extra virgin olive oil. Leave the peppers to marinate for 3 hours.

Toast the bread on a griddle and distribute the peppers between them. Serve at once.

◆

BRUSCHETTA CON SPINACI E POMODORI SECCHI

BRUSCHETTA WITH SPINACH AND SUN-DRIED TOMATOES

SERVES 4

4 slices of bread for bruschetta
900 g / 2 lb fresh spinach
2 tablespoons sun-dried tomatoes, cut in julienne
1½ tablespoons extra virgin olive oil
2 cloves garlic, finely chopped
salt and freshly ground black pepper

Thoroughly wash the spinach and remove the stalks. Cook the spinach with a little salt and only the water left on the leaves after washing. Drain and squeeze any excess water from the spinach.

Heat the olive oil in a frying pan over a medium heat, add the garlic and sun-dried tomatoes and briefly fry. Add the spinach and season with salt and freshly ground black pepper to taste.

Toast the bread on a griddle and spread with the spinach mixture. Serve at once.

◆

CROSTINI CON PASTA D'OLIVE

CROSTINI WITH OLIVE PASTE

This olive paste should be served in the same style as the French tepenade, brought to the table separately in a pot for each person to serve themselves crostini with an aperitif. Keep the bread warm in a folded cloth.

SERVES 4

slices of bread for crostini

200 g / 7 oz black olives, pitted

50 g / 1¾ oz salted capers

60 g / 2 oz anchovy fillets

2 tablespoons extra virgin olive oil

juice of 1 lemon

Rinse and dry the capers and put them in a food processor with the rest of the ingredients. Process until a smooth paste is obtained.

Toast the bread for the crostini under a grill [US broiler]. Serve the hot crostini and olive paste separately for everyone to spread their own.

◆

BRUSCHETTA ALL'UMBRA

BRUSCHETTA WITH GREEN OLIVES

These bruschetta are good as an accompaniment to
salami and prosciutto.

SERVES 4

4 slices of bread for bruschetta

4 tablespoons extra virgin olive oil

2 tablespoons fresh lemon juice

1 clove garlic, finely chopped

100 g / 3½ oz pitted green olives, roughly chopped

salt and freshly ground black pepper

Toast the bread on a griddle. At the same time heat the
olive oil with the lemon juice, garlic, olives, salt and
pepper, mixing the ingredients together. Spoon the olive
sauce over the bruschetta and serve at once.

◆

BRUSCHETTA CON VERDURE GRIGLIATE

BRUSCHETTA WITH GRILLED VEGETABLES

SERVES 4

4 slices of bread for bruschetta

2 zucchini

1 aubergine [US eggplant]

2 firm tomatoes

extra virgin olive oil, both plain and chilli-flavoured

fresh marjoram

garlic

salt

Slice the zucchini, aubergine and tomatoes and sprinkle
them with extra virgin olive oil. Cook on a very hot

griddle. Dress the vegetables with marjoram and finely chopped garlic and leave to marinate for an hour.

Toast the bread on a griddle and sprinkle with chilli-flavoured oil. Put the tomatoes on the bruschetta first of all, followed by the zucchini and aubergine. Do not lay them flat, but place them in a decorative way.

Serve immediately.

◆

CROSTINI AI FUNGHI PORCINI

CROSTINI WITH PORCINI MUSHROOMS

SERVES 4

12 slices of bread for crostini

milk to moisten bread

100 g / 3½ oz plain flour [US ⅔ cup all-purpose flour]

3 eggs, beaten

oil for frying

Mushroom topping

500 g / 1 lb fresh porcini (ceps)

2 tablespoons extra virgin olive oil

30 g / 1 oz [US 2 tablespoons] butter

2 cloves garlic, finely chopped

1 bunch of parsley, finely chopped

salt and freshly ground black pepper

Put the slices of bread on a tray and sprinkle with milk. Leave the crostini to rest for 1 hour.

Slice the mushrooms and fry them briskly in the oil and butter with the garlic. Add the parsley and season with salt and freshly ground black pepper. Keep in a warm place.

Dip the bread first in the flour and then in the beaten

eggs. Fry the crostini in abundant hot oil until golden brown on both sides. Drain on paper towels.

Top the crostini with the mushrooms and serve at once.

◆

CROSTINI CON PÂTÉ DI LENTICCHIE

CROSTINI WITH LENTIL PÂTÉ

SERVES 4

250 g/9 oz [US 1½ cups] Puy or Castelluccio lentils

1 carrot

1 stalk celery

1 onion

2 cloves garlic

1 tablespoon finely chopped parsley

4 tablespoons extra virgin olive oil

salt and freshly ground black pepper

slices of bread for crostini

Boil the lentils with the carrot, celery and onion in water to cover for 1 hour. Discard the vegetables, drain the lentils and purée them in a food processor. Add the crushed garlic, parsley, olive oil and seasoning to the mixture, stirring in well. Leave to rest for 2 hours before serving to allow the flavours to develop.

Toast the bread on a griddle under the grill [US broiler]. Bring the crostini and pâté separately to the table for everyone to help themselves.

◆

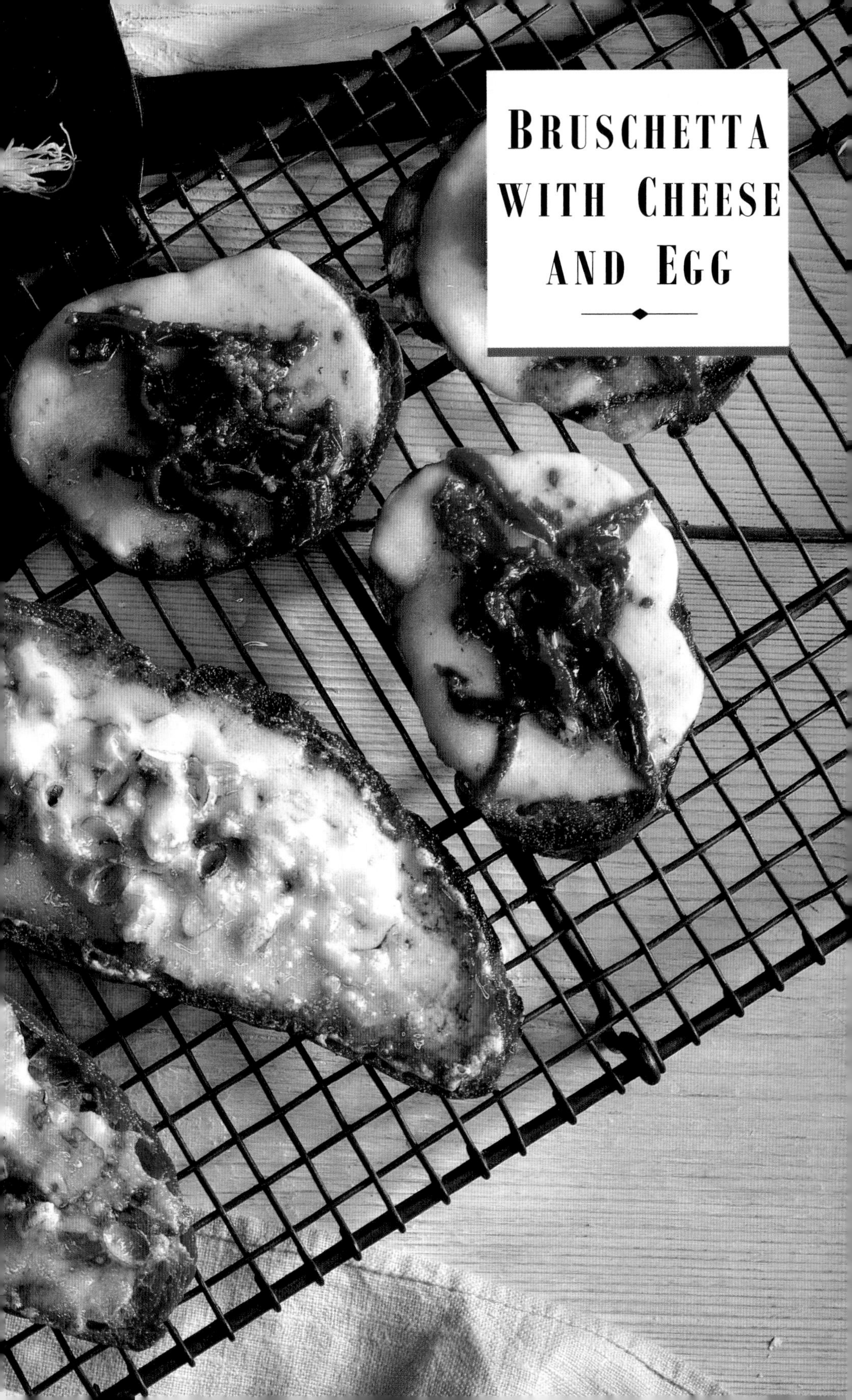

Bruschetta with Cheese and Egg

CROSTONI ALL'EMMENTAL E FUNGHI

CROSTONI OF EMMENTHAL AND MUSHROOMS

SERVES 4

4 slices of bread for crostoni

4 slices of emmenthal cheese

250 g/9 oz button mushrooms

extra virgin olive oil

2 cloves garlic, finely chopped

½ glass dry white wine

salt and freshly ground black pepper

nutmeg

*250 ml/9 fl oz [US 1 cup + 1 tablespoon] béchamel
sauce (page 37)*

4 tablespoons single cream [US light cream]

butter

4 slices of cooked ham

4 eggs

Slice the mushrooms. Heat 3 tablespoons of extra virgin olive oil, add the garlic and fry briefly, then add the mushrooms and fry. Add the wine and season with salt, freshly ground black pepper and a pinch of nutmeg. Reduce the wine to zero. Add the béchamel and the cream and cook for 10 minutes.

Butter the slices of bread and put on a buttered baking tray. Lay a slice of ham on each slice, then a slice of cheese and then the cheese sauce. Place the crostoni in an oven preheated to 200°C/400°F/gas 6. Meanwhile, poach the eggs.

Put an egg on the top of each crostoni when the sauce is golden and bubbling. Serve at once.

Previous pages:
Bruschetta with Fontina Cheese and Spring Onion (page 60)
Crostoni of Mozzarella and Anchovies (page 59)

CROSTONI DI FORMAGGIO ALLA VALDESE

CROSTONI OF EMMENTHAL

SERVES 4

4 slices of bread for crostoni

100 g/4 oz emmenthal cheese, grated

1 glass dry white wine

salt and freshly ground black pepper

1 egg

Toast the bread lightly under a grill [US broiler].

Mix the cheese with the white wine, mixing in thoroughly. Season with salt and freshly ground black pepper. Spread this mixture on the crostoni. Arrange on a baking tray.

Beat up the egg with a fork and pour over the cheese. Bake in an oven preheated to 220°C/425°F/gas 7 until the crostoni are golden brown. Serve immediately with pickled pear onions and gherkins.

◆

CROSTONI RUSTICI

RUSTIC CROSTONI

SERVES 4

8 slices of bread for crostoni

100 g/4 oz stracchino cheese

8 slices of Parma ham

Toast the bread on a griddle. Spread each crostoni with stracchino and put a slice of Parma ham on the top. Put the crostoni in a hot oven or under a grill [US broiler] and cook until the Parma ham is lightly crisped. Serve at once.

CROSTINI ALLA MOZZARELLA ALICI E POMODORI SECCHI

CROSTINI WITH MOZZARELLA, ANCHOVIES AND
SUN-DRIED TOMATOES

SERVES 6

12 slices of filone (page 19) for crostini
two 125g/5 oz mozzarella di bufala, cut in 12 slices
4 anchovy fillets, finely chopped
60 g/2 oz sun-dried tomatoes, cut in julienne
30 g/1 oz [US 2 tablespoons] unsalted butter
1 tablespoon extra virgin olive oil
2 cloves garlic, finely chopped

Preheat the grill [US broiler]

Toast the bread on a griddle and top each slice with a slice of mozzarella. Place under the grill and grill until the cheese is soft and melting.

While the cheese is cooking, heat the butter and oil in a small pan over a low heat. Add the garlic, anchovies and sun-dried tomatoes and cook, stirring constantly, for a minute or two.

Pour the garlic and anchovy mixture over the crostini and serve at once.

BRUSCHETTA AL CAPRINO E NOCI

BRUSCHETTA WITH GOAT'S CHEESE AND WALNUTS

SERVES 4

4 slices of bread for bruschetta
115 g/4 oz soft goat's cheese
16 walnut halves, roughly chopped
2 tablespoons finely chopped parsley

Lightly toast the bread on a griddle or under a grill [US broiler].

Mix the parsley with the goat's cheese and spread on the toast. Sprinkle the walnuts on top and serve at once.

◆

CROSTINI DI MOZZARELLA E ALICI

CROSTINI OF MOZZARELLA AND ANCHOVIES

SERVES 4

8 slices of bread for crostini
300 g/10 oz mozzarella cheese, cut in 8 slices
100 g/4 oz [US ½ cup] butter
4 anchovy fillets, mashed with a fork
salt and freshly ground black pepper

Preheat the grill [US broiler].

Toast the crostini on a griddle. Put a slice of mozzarella on top of each one and season with salt and freshly ground black pepper. Place under the heated grill to melt the cheese.

Heat the butter and just as it starts to foam add the anchovies, stirring in well with a wooden spoon. Remove from the heat.

When the mozzarella is cooked, pour the anchovy butter over the crostini. Serve at once.

CROSTINI CON FORMAGGIO DI CAPRA

CROSTINI WITH GOAT'S CHEESE

A light mixed leaf salad would make a perfect
accompaniment to these crostini.

SERVES 4

4 slices of bread for crostini

*4 slices 2.5 cm / 1 in thick of goat's cheese, cut from
6 cm / 2½ in diameter log-type goat's cheese (chèvre)*

extra virgin olive oil

freshly ground black pepper

white truffle or summer truffle (optional)

Toast the bread under a grill [US broiler] on one side
only. Place a slice of goat's cheese on the untoasted side
of each crostini. Drizzle a little olive oil over the cheese
and season with freshly ground black pepper. Place under
the grill and cook until the cheese is warmed through. Do
not allow the cheese to colour.

A few shavings of white truffle or summer truffle are a
perfect addition to this dish if they are available.

◆

BRUSCHETTA CON FORMAGGIO FONTINA E CIPOLLINA

BRUSCHETTA WITH FONTINA CHEESE AND SPRING ONION

SERVES 4

4 slices of bread for bruschetta

4 thin slices of fontina cheese

1 clove garlic

4 tablespoons finely chopped spring onion [US scallion]

4 tablespoons extra virgin olive oil

Toast the bread on a griddle. Rub the bread with the
garlic, drizzle the oil over and sprinkle the bread with the
spring onion. Place the fontina cheese on top.

Place the bruschetta under a preheated grill [US broiler] until the cheese is warmed through. Serve at once.

CROSTINI CON FONTINA E TARTUFI

CROSTINI WITH FONTINA AND TRUFFLES

Black truffle, which has been sliced and quickly sautéed in butter, will do as a substitute if a white truffle is not available.

SERVES 4

4 slices of bread for crostini

4 slices of fontina cheese (the same size as the bread)

1 white truffle

truffle oil

Toast the crostini lightly under a grill [US broiler]. Drizzle a little truffle oil over them. Place a slice of fontina cheese on top and place under the grill. When the cheese is soft, remove from the heat, drizzle a little more truffle oil on top and decorate with a slice or two of white truffle.

UOVA CON FUNGHI SU CROSTINI

CROSTINI WITH EGG AND MUSHROOMS

SERVES 4

4 slices of bread for crostini

300 g/10 oz fresh porcini (ceps) or shiitake mushrooms

4 eggs

extra virgin olive oil

salt and freshly ground white pepper

finely chopped parsley

white wine vinegar

Slice the mushrooms and fry them in a little olive oil. Season with salt and freshly ground white pepper. Add

the parsley at the last minute. Toast the bread on a griddle. Poach the eggs lightly in water with a teaspoon of white wine vinegar added.

Divide the mushrooms among the crostini, place a poached egg on top and sprinkle with freshly ground white pepper and a little more parsley. Serve at once.

◆

CROSTINI ALLA VALDOSTANA

CROSTINI WITH FONTINA

SERVES 4

8 slices of bread for crostini

150 g / 5 oz fontina cheese

30 g / 1 oz dried porcini

2 tablespoons extra virgin olive oil

2 cloves garlic, finely chopped

3 tablespoons dry white wine

salt and freshly ground black pepper

1 tablespoon finely chopped parsley

Soak the mushrooms in hot water for half an hour. Wash them thoroughly and dry them. Chop the mushrooms roughly.

Heat the oil in a frying pan, add the garlic and mushrooms and cook for 20 minutes over a low heat. Add the wine after 10 minutes of cooking. When the mushrooms are cooked, season with salt and freshly ground black pepper and add the parsley.

Chop the fontina cheese into small cubes.

Toast the bread on a griddle. Divide the cheese among the crostini, put the mushrooms on top and place in an oven preheated to 200°C/400°F/gas 6 for a few minutes.

Previous pages:
Crostoni with Egg and Lentils (page 66)

CROSTINI DI RICOTTA E NOCI

CROSTINI OF RICOTTA WITH WALNUTS

SERVES 6

18 slices of bread for crostini
120 g/4 oz ricotta cheese
200 g/7 oz mascarpone
2 tablespoons olive oil
salt and freshly ground black pepper
24 walnut halves, roughly chopped

Toast the bread lightly under a grill [US broiler]. Mix together the ricotta, mascarpone, olive oil, salt and a generous amount of freshly ground black pepper. Spread the cheese mixture over the crostini and sprinkle with the roughly chopped walnuts. Serve at once.

◆

CROSTONI CON UOVA E FORMAGGIO

CROSTONI WITH EGG AND CHEESE

SERVES 4

4 slices of bread for crostoni
8 eggs
salt and freshly ground white pepper
40 g/1½ oz Parmesan cheese, freshly grated
100 g/4 oz Bel Paese cheese, cut in small cubes
20 g/¾ oz [US 1½ tablespoons] butter

Beat the eggs with salt and pepper. Add the Parmesan cheese and the Bel Paese. Heat the butter in a non-stick frying pan, add the egg mixture and cook lightly, mixing with a fork.

Toast the bread on a griddle. Put the egg mixture on the crostoni. Serve at once.

CROSTONI CON UOVA E LENTICCHIE

CROSTONI WITH EGG AND LENTILS

SERVES 4

4 slices of bread for crostoni

120 g/4½ oz [US ⅔ cup] lentils, Puy or Castelluccio

4 eggs

50 g/1¾ oz [US ½ cup] in total of very finely chopped carrot, celery and onion

extra virgin olive oil

100 g/4 oz [US ½ cup] tomato coulis (page 67) or tomato passata

300 ml/½ pt [US 1¼ cups] boiling stock

salt and freshly ground black pepper

150 g/5 oz button mushrooms

vinegar

finely chopped parsley

Put the lentils to soak the evening before in tepid water.

Fry the finely chopped carrot, celery and onion in 2 table-spoons of extra virgin olive oil. Add the lentils, well drained. Stir for 1 or 2 minutes, then add the tomato coulis and the boiling stock. Lightly season with salt and pepper. Bring the lentils to the boil, then lower the heat, cover the pan and gently cook for about 25 minutes.

In the meantime slice the mushrooms and fry in 2 table-spoons of extra virgin olive oil. Bring to the boil 1 litre/1¾ pints [US 1 quart] of water in a frying pan with a tablespoon of vinegar. Poach the eggs for 4 minutes. Toast the slices of bread on a griddle.

Divide the lentils among the crostoni, then add the mushrooms and finally the poached egg. Serve at once, sprinkled with parsley and freshly ground black pepper.

◆

CROSTONI CON UOVA FRITTE E FONTINA

CROSTONI WITH FRIED EGG AND FONTINA

SERVES 4

4 slices of bread for crostoni

4 eggs

4 slices of fontina cheese

8 anchovy fillets

freshly ground black pepper

butter

Toast the slices of bread under a grill [US broiler]. Place a slice of fontina on each crostoni and then a fillet of anchovy on top of the cheese and season with freshly ground black pepper. Place the crostoni under a medium grill so that the cheese melts gently.

As the cheese is melting fry the eggs in a little butter. Place a fried egg on top of each crostoni.

Quickly melt a bit of butter in a small frying pan and add the other 4 anchovies. Break them up with a fork until they form a sauce. Pour this anchovy butter over the eggs and serve at once.

◆

TOMATO COULIS

MAKES 450 ML / ¾ PT [US 2 CUPS]

500 g / 1 lb 2 oz very ripe plum tomatoes

1 tablespoon finely chopped onion

1 tablespoon finely chopped garlic

1 tablespoon extra virgin olive oil

salt and freshly ground black pepper

Roughly chop the tomatoes. Gently fry the onion and garlic in the olive oil until soft and golden, then add the tomatoes and cook until soft. Season with salt and freshly ground black pepper. Pass the tomato mixture through the fine holes of a vegetable mill.

CROSTONI CON UOVA AL PROSCIUTTO

CROSTONI WITH EGG AND PROSCIUTTO

SERVES 4

4 slices of bread for crostoni

6 eggs

2 tablespoons freshly grated Parmesan cheese

2 tablespoons single cream [US light cream]

salt and freshly ground black pepper

75 g/2½ oz [US 5 tablespoons] butter

100 g/4 oz Parma ham, cut in julienne

piquant paprika

Toast the bread on a griddle and butter them using 50 g/1¾ oz [US 3½ tablespoons] of the butter.

Break the eggs into a bowl. Add the Parmesan, cream, salt and pepper and beat well with a fork. In a non-stick pan, melt the remaining butter, add the eggs and scramble them for a few minutes, stirring always with a wooden spoon. At the last minute add the Parma ham and stir in.

Divide the egg and ham mixture among the crostoni and sprinkle a little piquant paprika on top. Serve at once.

◆

CROSTONI INTEGRALI CON UOVA E GORGONZOLA

WHOLEMEAL BREAD CROSTONI WITH EGG AND GORGONZOLA

SERVES 4

4 large slices of wholemeal bread for crostoni

4 eggs

125 g/4½ oz gorgonzola cheese

Previous pages:
Wholemeal Bread Crostoni with Egg and Gorgonzola (page 70)
Crostini with Goat's Cheese (page 60)

butter

salt and freshly ground black pepper

1 tablespoon finely chopped parsley

Melt 60 g/2 oz [US 4 tablespoons] of butter. Brush each slice of bread with the melted butter. Place the bread on a baking tray and put in a preheated oven set at 230°C/450°F/gas 8 to toast for 4–5 minutes.

Meanwhile, beat the eggs with a small piece of butter, a pinch of salt and a pinch of freshly grated black pepper. Scramble the eggs in a bain marie over a medium heat; they must remain soft.

Remove the crostoni from the oven. Spread the gorgonzola on them while they are still hot, then spoon the scrambled eggs on top. Sprinkle the parsley over and serve at once.

CROSTINI AL GORGONZOLA

CROSTINI WITH GORGONZOLA

SERVES 4

4 slices of bread for crostini

115g/4 oz sweet gorgonzola cheese

3 tablespoons mascarpone

1 ripe pear

Bake the crostini in a preheated medium oven until they are golden. Leave to cool.

Mix the gorgonzola and the mascarpone together with a wooden spoon until a soft cream is obtained. When the crostini are cold, spread with the cheese mixture.

Peel and thinly slice the pear. Put a slice or two of pear on top of each crostini.

FISH AND SHELLFISH BRUSCHETTA

◆

Bruschetta con Frutti di Mare

BRUSCHETTA WITH SEAFOOD

SERVES 4

4 slices of bread for bruschetta

500 g / 1 lb 2 oz fresh mussels

60 g / 2 oz cooked squid, cut in rings

16 cooked peeled prawns [US small shrimp]

6 anchovy fillets, roughly chopped

3 cloves garlic, 2 of them finely chopped and 1 halved

1 tablespoon finely chopped parsley

extra virgin olive oil

20 g / ¾ oz sun-dried tomatoes in olive oil, cut in julienne

30 black olives, pitted

salt and freshly ground black pepper

1 generous pinch dried hot chilli flakes

8 fresh basil leaves

Wash the mussels and remove the beards. Place them in a shallow pan, cover the pan and leave over high heat until they have opened. Remove the mussels from the shells, reserving 4 in their shell for decoration. Strain and reserve the mussel liquor.

Toast the bread on a griddle, rub with garlic and dress with olive oil. Keep warm.

Fry the chopped garlic and parsley briefly in 2 table-spoons olive oil. Add the sun-dried tomatoes and the olives and fry for a few seconds. Add 2 tablespoons of the mussel liquor.

Add all the fish, warm them through and season with salt, pepper and chilli flakes. Serve on the bruschetta. Decorate each with shreds of fresh basil and a mussel in shell.

Previous pages:
Bruschetta with Seafood (page 74)
Crostini with Stuffed Squid (page 84)

CROSTINI ALLA PESCATORA

FISHERMAN'S CROSTINI

SERVES 6

12 slices of bread for crostini
24 fresh mussels
4 anchovy fillets, finely chopped
4 tablespoons extra virgin olive oil
1 clove garlic, finely chopped
2 tablespoons finely chopped parsley
breadcrumbs
freshly ground black pepper

Thoroughly clean the mussels under cold running water, removing the beards.

Heat the olive oil in a frying pan and stir in the garlic, parsley and anchovies. Add the mussels, raise the heat, cover the pan and cook until the mussels are open. Remove the mussels from the pan and reserve. Reduce the pan liquids until the watery part has evaporated.

Remove one half of each mussel shell. Put a pinch of breadcrumbs on top of each mussel and pass under a hot grill [US broiler] for a few minutes.

Toast the bread on a griddle. Put 2 mussels on each slice and pour the cooking juices over. Season with freshly ground black pepper to taste and serve at once.

Overleaf:
Squid in Tomato Sauce on Crostini (page 85)
Crostini with Anchovies (page 87)
Polenta Bruschetta with Salt Cod (page 146)
Crostini with Mussels (page 81)

BRUSCHETTA DI ARRAGOSTA ALLA SARDA

BRUSCHETTA OF LOBSTER THE SARDINIAN WAY

Dublin Bay Prawns can be used for this recipe instead
of the lobster.

SERVES 6

6 slices of bread for bruschetta

2 live lobsters, 800 g / 1¾ lb each

4 cloves garlic

2 large dried hot chilli peppers

4 tablespoons extra virgin olive oil

1 glass dry white wine

*12 sun-dried tomato halves preserved in oil, 2 of them
cut in julienne*

1 large ladle fresh tomato coulis (page 67)

or tomato passata

750 ml / 1¼ pt [US 3 cups] water

4 plum tomatoes, peeled, seeded and diced

salt and freshly ground black pepper

finely shredded fresh basil leaves, to decorate

Put the lobsters in boiling salted water and boil for 3 minutes. Remove from the heat and leave to stand for 5
minutes. Take the lobsters from the water. Remove the
meat from the body and cut into medallions, making sure
you discard the stomach and sandbag. Crack the claws
and remove the meat.

Fry the whole garlic cloves and whole chilli peppers in
the olive oil until the garlic is golden. Add the white wine,
dried tomato halves, tomato coulis and the water. Bring
the mixture to the boil, then lower the heat and simmer
for 20 minutes.

Remove the mixture from the heat. Discard the garlic
and chillies and blend all the rest together in a blender
until a smooth sauce is obtained. Return the sauce to a
non-stick frying pan, add the julienne of dried tomato and

the concassé of fresh tomato and season with salt and freshly ground black pepper. Bring the sauce gently back to simmering. Add the lobster pieces and warm through.

Toast the bread on a griddle. Serve the lobster and sauce spooned over the bruschetta, decorated with shredded basil. Serve at once.

BRUSCHETTA CON TELLINE ALLA NAPOLETANA

BRUSCHETTA WITH COCKLES NAPOLETANA

Vongole (clams) can also be used.

SERVES 4

4 slices of bread for bruschetta

1 kg/2¼ lb live cockles

400 g/14 oz plum tomatoes, peeled, seeded and chopped

100 ml/4 fl oz [US ½ cup] extra virgin olive oil

2 cloves garlic, finely chopped

1 small bunch of parsley, finely chopped

salt and freshly ground black pepper

Wash the cockles thoroughly. Leave them covered in cold salted water for 1 hour, stirring occasionally, to purge the sand.

Drain the cockles, place in a large pan and put on the heat. When the shells have all opened remove the cockles from their shells. Strain the liquor from the cockles, reduce by half and reserve.

Heat the olive oil in a frying pan, add the garlic and parsley and briefly fry, then add the tomatoes and gently cook for 10 minutes. Add the cockle liquor and the cockles and briefly bring to the boil. Season with salt and pepper.

Toast the bread on a griddle and spoon the cockles in sauce over the top. Serve at once.

CROSTINI DI TELLINE

CROSTINI OF COCKLES

SERVES 4

12 slices of bread for crostini
100 g/4 oz steamed shelled cockles
20 g/¾ oz salted capers, well rinsed and dried
40 g/1½ oz [US ½ cup] pine nuts
extra virgin olive oil
a dash of white wine vinegar
salt and pepper
2 eggs, beaten with a little milk
finely chopped parsley
dry breadcrumbs
light olive oil

Finely chop the cockles. Add the capers and the pine nuts, chopped as well. Dress with extra virgin olive oil, a little white wine vinegar, salt and pepper. Mix everything well together.

Dip the bread in the beaten egg and milk to which a little chopped parsley has been added, then dip in breadcrumbs to coat. Fry the crostini in light olive oil.

Spoon the cockle mixture on top of the hot crostini and serve.

◆

BRUSCHETTA DI TELLINE

BRUSCHETTA WITH COCKLES

SERVES 4

4 slices of bread for bruschetta
1 kg/2¼ lb live cockles, well washed
2 cloves garlic
extra virgin olive oil
1 large dried hot red chilli pepper

3½ tablespoons dry white wine
juice of ½ lemon

Purge the cockles (see page 79). Put them in a large pan and place on a strong heat. Remove the cockles from the pan as soon as they open. Take the cockles from their shells; strain the liquor and reserve it.

Toast the slices of bread on a griddle and rub with one of the garlic cloves. Keep warm.

Heat 2 tablespoons of olive oil and fry the remaining garlic clove and the chilli. When the garlic is a golden colour, discard it. Add the cockles and cook for an instant or two, then add the white wine, lemon juice and the cockle liquor. After a few minutes cooking, spoon the cockles on to the bruschetta. Serve at once.

CROSTINI CON COZZE

CROSTINI WITH MUSSELS

SERVES 4

8 slices of bread for crostini
40 fresh mussels, scrubbed
120 ml/4 fl oz [US ½ cup] thick tomato coulis
(page 67) seasoned with extra garlic and chilli flakes
to taste
finely chopped parsley

Place the mussels in a large shallow pan, so that they are only in one layer. Put the pan on the heat, cover and leave the mussels to open. Remove the mussels from the shells, but reserve 8 in their shells for decoration. Add the mussels to the thick tomato coulis which has been extra seasoned and warmed.

Toast the bread on a griddle. Reheat the mussels and spoon the mixture on to the crostini. Sprinkle with finely chopped parsley and garnish each crostini with a mussel in its shell. Serve at once.

CROSTONI DI CALAMARI

SQUID CROSTONI

SERVES 6

6 slices of bread for crostoni

6 squid, 100g / 3½ oz each

6 tablespoons olive oil

grated zest of 1 lemon

juice of 2 lemons

1 clove garlic, finely chopped

2 small hot red chilli peppers, seeded and finely chopped

1 tablespoon finely chopped Italian (flat) parsley

salt and freshly ground black pepper

To clean the squid, detach the head; as you pull it off, the interior of the body comes away too. Insert your fingers in the body and remove the quill and any soft material left inside. Pull the purple coloured skin off the body – it comes away very easily. Do all this process under a gently running cold tap. Remove the two fins and skin them as well. Cut the tentacles off just in front of the eyes. Remove the beak-like mouth from the centre of the tentacles and discard it. Remove the skin from the tentacles as well as you can.

Split the body down one side and pass once more under a running tap, to make sure it is absolutely clean. Now flatten the squid on a board with the outer side facing up. With a very sharp knife score 1.5 cm/½ in lines diagonally, cutting half-way through the flesh, then cut the other way so you obtain diamond shapes all over the surface. Do the same to the fins.

Place the tentacles, fins and body in a bowl. Add the olive oil, lemon zest and juice, garlic, chilli pepper, parsley, salt and freshly ground black pepper and mix in well. Leave to marinate for at least 1 hour.

Heat a griddle until very hot. Place the bodies on the griddle, scored sides down, and add the fins and tentacles.

After 30 seconds turn the pieces over and cook for another 30 seconds or longer if needed. When cooked curl up the body in its original form.

Toast the bread for the crostoni on the griddle. Place the squid on top and spoon some of the marinade over to soak into the crostoni. Serve at once.

CROSTONI MARINARI

SAILOR'S CROSTONI

SERVES 6

6 slices of bread for crostoni
550 g / 1¼ lb live cockles, well washed and purged
(page 79)
300 g / 10 oz plum tomatoes, peeled and seeded
1 small handful of fresh basil leaves
extra virgin olive oil
salt and freshly ground black pepper
2 cloves garlic, 1 of them finely chopped
1 tablespoon finely chopped parsley

Cut the tomatoes into small cubes. Put them in a shallow dish and dress with the basil roughly shredded, 2 table-spoons of extra virgin olive oil, salt and freshly ground black pepper. Cover the dish with some film and leave at room temperature for half an hour.

Put the cockles in a large frying pan with 1 tablespoon of extra virgin olive oil and the whole clove of garlic. As soon as the cockles are open remove them from the pan and take them out of their shells. Dress with a little extra virgin olive oil.

Toast the bread on a griddle and rub with the finely chopped garlic. Spoon the tomatoes on top of the crostoni and then the cockles and sprinkle with a little finely chopped parsley. Serve at once.

CROSTINI CON CALAMARI RIPIENI

CROSTINI WITH STUFFED SQUID

SERVES 6

6 slices of bread for crostini
1 kg/2¼ lb small squid
50 g/1¾ oz [US cup] fresh breadcrumbs
4 salted anchovies, rinsed, dried and finely chopped
2 cloves garlic, finely chopped
2 tablespoons finely chopped parsley
salt and freshly ground black pepper
5 tablespoons extra virgin olive oil
90 ml/3 fl oz [US 6 tablespoons] dry white wine
6 wedges of lemon

Clean the squid (see page 82). Leave the body intact, making sure it is well cleaned inside by turning it inside out and rinsing under cold water. Return the body to the correct way.

Mix the breadcrumbs with the anchovies, garlic, parsley and freshly ground black pepper. Stuff the squid with this mixture and close the opening with a wooden cocktail stick.

Place the stuffed squid and tentacles in a terracotta dish. Pour the olive oil and dry white wine over them and add a pinch of salt. Bake in an oven preheated to 230°C/450°F/gas 8 for 20 minutes.

Toast the bread on a griddle. Serve the stuffed squid and tentacles on top of the crostini, with some of the cooking juices poured over and with a wedge of lemon.

CALAMARI IN UMIDO SU CROSTINI

SQUID IN TOMATO SAUCE ON CROSTINI

SERVES 10

10 slices of bread for crostini

450 g / 1 lb cleaned small squid

5 tablespoons extra virgin olive oil plus extra for dribbling on the crostini

1 clove garlic, finely chopped

3 tablespoons dry white wine

400 g / 14 oz plum tomatoes, peeled, seeded and roughly chopped

salt and freshly ground black pepper

1 tablespoon finely chopped parsley

When cleaning the squid (see page 82), leave the bodies intact.

Heat the olive oil in a frying pan, add the garlic and fry. Add the squid bodies and tentacles and, over a medium heat, 'dry' the squid – a lot of liquid will come out of the squid which must be evaporated. Now add the dry white wine and reduce it to almost nothing. Add the tomato pulp, season generously with salt and pepper and add two-thirds of the parsley. Bring to the boil, then reduce the heat and cook for 30 minutes, stirring from time to time. Add a little water if you see the sauce drying out too much.

Serve on hot crostini, either fried in olive oil or toasted on the griddle, with olive oil dribbled over. Sprinkle the remaining parsley on top and serve at once.

◆

CROSTINI DI ACCIUGHE CON I FICHI

CROSTINI WITH ANCHOVIES AND FIGS

This is an unusual but good combination of flavours. It is a very old Corsican recipe.

SERVES 4

8 slices of bread for crostini

12 ripe figs

4 anchovy fillets, roughly chopped

1 clove garlic, roughly chopped

extra virgin olive oil

Peel the figs and process them to a purée with the anchovies and garlic.

Toast the bread lightly on a griddle and sprinkle with extra virgin olive oil. Spread the crostini with the fig mixture and serve.

◆

PANE CONDITO

TASTY BREAD

SERVES 4

4 slices of bread

extra virgin olive oil

dried oregano

8 salted anchovies, well rinsed, dried and finely chopped

12 black olives, pitted and sliced

freshly ground black pepper to taste

Toast the bread on a griddle.

Sprinkle the toast with extra virgin olive oil, then dress with oregano, finely chopped anchovies, sliced black olives and freshly ground black pepper. Serve at once.

CROSTINI DI ALICI

CROSTINI WITH ANCHOVIES

This recipe comes from the Abruzzi coast, hence the use of chilli pepper. These anchovies are 'cooked' only by the marinade and must be left whole.

SERVES 4

4 slices of bread for crostini

250 g/9 oz fresh anchovies

250 ml/8 fl oz [US 1 cup] white wine vinegar

1 clove garlic, finely chopped

1 tablespoon dried oregano

90 ml/3 fl oz [US 6 tablespoons] extra virgin olive oil

salt

freshly ground dried chilli pepper to taste or 1 small fresh hot chilli pepper, seeded and finely chopped

Clean and bone the anchovies and place them in a deep dish. Pour the vinegar over them and leave them to marinate for 10 minutes.

Drain the anchovies thoroughly and put them on a plate. Sprinkle with the garlic, oregano, olive oil, salt and chilli.

Toast the bread on a griddle. While the bread is still hot divide the anchovies among the crostini and pour any excess oil mixture on top. Serve at once.

Overleaf:
Grilled Sardine on Bruschetta (page 90)

SARDE ALLA CETRARESE SU BRUSCHETTA

GRILLED SARDINE ON BRUSCHETTA

SERVES 4

4 slices of bread for bruschetta

8 fresh sardines, boned

extra virgin olive oil

salt and freshly ground black pepper

dried oregano

garlic

4 wedges of lemon

Heat a grill [US broiler]. Place the sardines on a baking tray and sprinkle with olive oil, a little salt and dried oregano inside and outside. Place under the grill. When cooked on the upper side turn them gently over and finish the cooking.

Toast the bread on a griddle and rub with garlic. Serve the sardines on the bruschetta, two per each slice of bread. Pour a little of the cooking juices over the fish and serve at once, with lemon wedges.

◆

BRUSCHETTA CON ARINGHE ALLA CALABRESE

BRUSCHETTA WITH HERRINGS CALABRESE

SERVES 4

4 slices of bread for bruschetta

800 g / 1¾ lb fresh herrings, filleted

2 tablespoons extra virgin olive oil

1 clove garlic, finely chopped

1 small hot red chilli pepper, seeded and finely chopped

salt

Heat the oil in a frying pan, add the garlic and fry briefly. Add the herring fillets and chilli and season lightly with a little salt. Cook over a low heat until the herring is reduced to a pulp.

Toast the bread on a griddle and spread the herring mixture on top. Serve at once.

BRUSCHETTA DI PESCE SPADA

BRUSCHETTA WITH SWORDFISH

SERVES 6

6 slices of bread for bruschetta
270 g / 9¾ oz swordfish, cut in 18 small slices
300 g / 10 oz cleaned leeks
extra virgin olive oil
dry white wine
salt and freshly ground black pepper
dried thyme
balsamic vinegar

Cut the leeks in rings and put them in a saucepan with 1 tablespoon of extra virgin olive oil, 170 ml/6 fl oz [US ¾ cup] water, a couple of tablespoons of dry white wine and a pinch of salt. Cook, covered, over a moderate heat until the leeks are softened. Blend the leek mixture with 2 tablespoons of extra virgin olive oil until a dense smooth purée is obtained.

Place the slices of swordfish on a non-stick baking tray and season with salt, freshly ground black pepper, thyme and extra virgin olive oil. Place the tray of fish in an oven preheated to 200°C/400°F/ gas 6 to cook for 3–4 minutes.

Toast the bread on a griddle and sprinkle with a little extra virgin olive oil. Spread the leek purée on top and place the slices of swordfish on the bruschetta. Sprinkle a little more thyme, olive oil and a few drops of balsamic vinegar on each. Serve at once.

CROSTINI ALL'ARINGA

CROSTINI WITH HERRINGS

SERVES 4

4 slices of bread for crostini

400 g/14 oz smoked herrings

milk

1 apple

1 onion

1 slice of dry bread (no crust)

white wine vinegar

salt and freshly ground black pepper

olive oil

Leave the herrings to soak in milk for 6 hours.

Peel, core and finely chop the apple. Finely chop the onion. Soak the slice of bread in a little milk and squeeze it dry. Process the drained herrings, apple, onion and bread to a paste. Season with a few drops of vinegar, salt and freshly ground black pepper.

Toast the bread on a griddle and drizzle with olive oil. Spread the herring paste on top and serve.

◆

CROSTINI DI CREMA AL TONNO

CROSTINI WITH TUNA PURÉE

SERVES 4

4 slices of bread for crostini

170 g/6 oz canned tuna

1 tablespoon salted capers, rinsed and dried

4 anchovy fillets

Previous pages:
Crostini with Avocado and Prawns (page 96)
Bruschetta of Lobster the Sardinian Way (page 78)

6 tablespoons mayonnaise

juice of 1 lemon

1 tablespoon finely chopped parsley

Process the tuna, capers and anchovies together. Mix in the mayonnaise and add the lemon juice and parsley.

Toast the bread on a griddle and spread with the tuna mixture. Serve.

CROSTINI ALLA TAPENADE

CROSTINI WITH TAPENADE

SERVES 6

6 slices of bread for crostini

2 heaped tablespoons salted capers

24 black olives, pitted

8 anchovy fillets

60 g / 2 oz canned tuna fish (under oil), drained

4 tablespoons extra virgin olive oil

2 tablespoons lemon juice

freshly ground black pepper

6 hard-boiled eggs, sliced

1 tablespoon finely chopped parsley, to decorate

Rinse the capers thoroughly and dry them. Put the capers, olives, anchovies and tuna into a food processor. Process until smooth. Add the extra virgin olive oil a little at a time while processing. Add the lemon juice and season with freshly ground black pepper.

Toast the bread on a griddle. Spread the tapenade on top and layer the slices of egg on top of the tapenade. Sprinkle the egg with finely chopped parsley and serve at once.

CROSTINI ALL'AVOCADO E GAMBERI

CROSTINI WITH AVOCADO AND PRAWNS

If the avocado mixture is not going to be used immediately, place an avocado stone in the middle of the sauce to prevent it from going black. Cover tightly with clingfilm until required.

SERVES 4

4 slices of bread for crostini

2 medium avocados

8 large cooked prawns [US large shrimp]

50 g | 1¾ oz [US 3½ tablespoons] mascarpone

juice of ½ lemon

salt and freshly ground white pepper

1 tablespoon finely chopped chives

Process the avocado pulp with the mascarpone. Season with lemon juice, salt and freshly ground white pepper.

Lightly toast the bread under a grill [US broiler]. Spread the avocado mixture on each toast and place 2 peeled prawns on top. Sprinkle with a little finely chopped chives. Serve at once.

◆

CROSTINI CON MASCARPONE E SALMONE AFFUMICATO

CROSTINI WITH MASCARPONE AND SMOKED SALMON

SERVES 4

8 slices of bread for crostini

8 level tablespoons of mascarpone

8 slices of smoked salmon (same sizes as the crostini)

cayenne pepper

chopped chives

lemon wedges

Toast the bread on a griddle. Spread 1 tablespoon of mascarpone on each slice, place the smoked salmon lightly on top and sprinkle with cayenne pepper and chopped chives. Serve with lemon wedges.

CROSTONI CON SARDINE E CIPOLLE MARINATE

CROSTONI WITH MARINATED ONIONS AND SARDINES

SERVES 4

4 slices of bread for crostoni
4 canned sardines (under olive oil)
1 red onion
white wine vinegar
white wine
salt and a few grains of black pepper
1 bay leaf
extra virgin olive oil
1 tablespoon finely chopped parsley

Peel the onion and slice very thinly. Put it in a bowl. Combine half a glass of white wine vinegar, half a glass of white wine, a pinch of salt, a few grains of pepper and a bay leaf in a saucepan and bring to the boil. Pour the boiling vinegar and wine mixture over the onions. Leave the onions to marinate for 1 hour, then drain and dress with a little olive oil.

Toast the bread on a griddle. Divide the onions among the crostoni and place a sardine on top. Sprinkle with finely chopped parsley and serve.

CROSTINI CON SALMONE AFFUMICATO E PEPE VERDE

CROSTINI WITH SMOKED SALMON AND GREEN PEPPERCORNS

SERVES 4

8 slices of bread for crostini

8 slices of smoked salmon, (same size as the crostini)

*2 fresh soft goat's cheese, each weighing approximately
100 g/4 oz*

2 spring onions [US scallions], finely chopped

2 tablespoons finely chopped parsley

4 green peppercorns preserved in brine

salt

olive oil

fresh dill

Mix the goat's cheese with spring onions, parsley, mashed peppercorns, a pinch of salt and a drop of olive oil.

Toast the bread under the grill [US broiler]. Spread the cheese mixture on top and put a slice of smoked salmon on each crostini. Decorate each with a little sprig of dill.

Bruschetta con crema di tonno e alici

BRUSCHETTA WITH TUNA AND ANCHOVIES

Serves 4

4 slices of bread for bruschetta
1 can tuna in olive oil, drained
1 can mackerel in oil, drained
1 can anchovy fillets, drained
30 g / 1 oz [US 2 tablespoons] butter
1 tablespoon finely chopped parsley
1 tablespoon finely chopped fresh basil
1 pinch hot paprika
salt and freshly ground black pepper

Combine the tuna, half of the mackerel, 3 of the anchovies and the butter in a food processor and process until smooth. Add the parsley, basil and pinch of paprika. Season with salt and freshly ground black pepper.

Toast the bread under the grill [US broiler]. Spread it with the fish mixture and decorate with the remaining mackerel and anchovies.

◆

Meat, Offal and Game Bruschetta

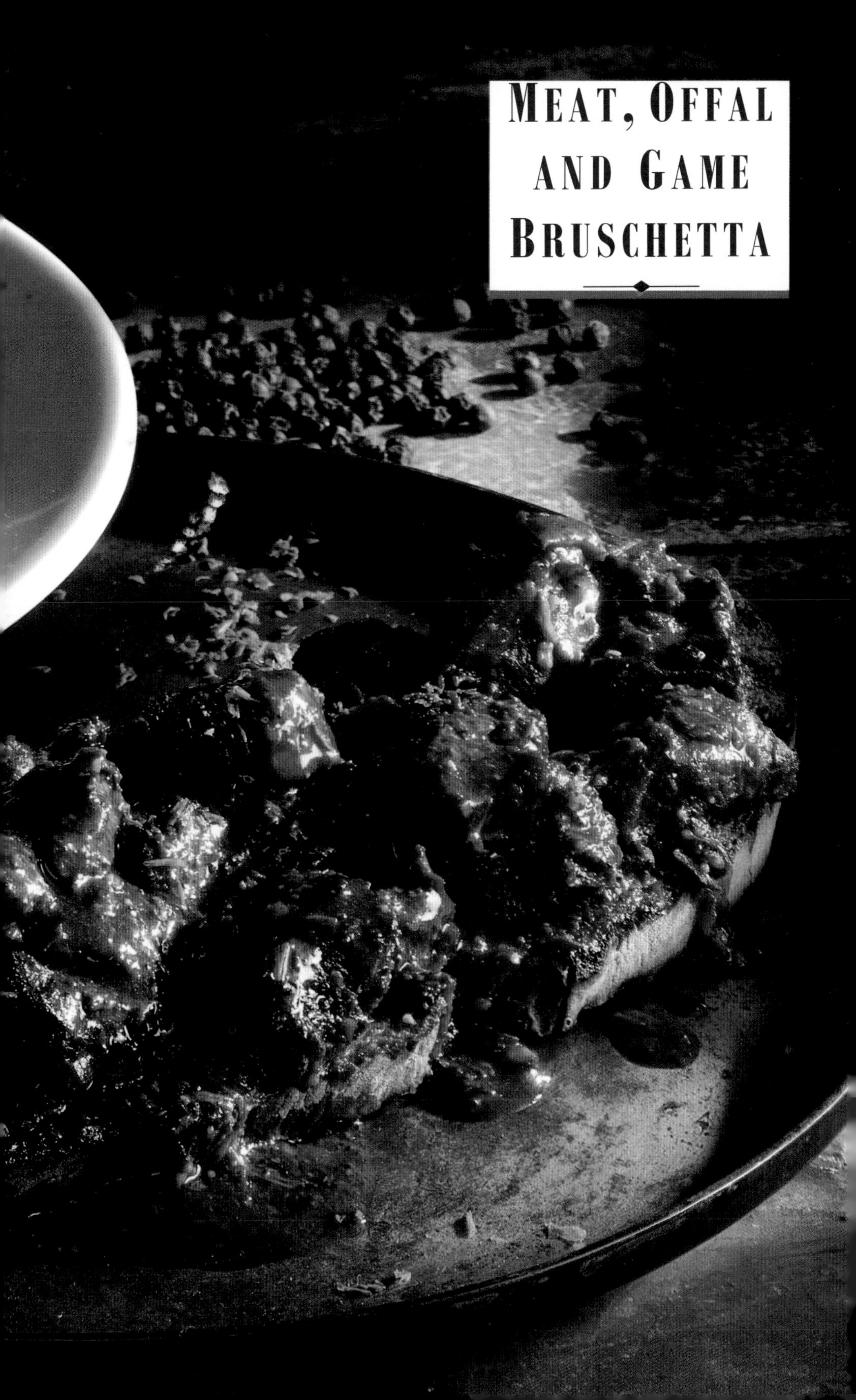

CROSTINI CON PEPERONI E SALSICCE

CROSTINI WITH PEPPERS AND SAUSAGE

SERVES 12 AS ANTIPASTO 6 AS A MAIN COURSE

12 slices of bread for crostini

6 red sweet peppers

360 g/12 oz Marchigiani sausages (page 103)

100 g/4 oz fresh breadcrumbs

400 ml/14 fl oz milk

2 eggs

2 tablespoons fresh breadcrumbs

extra virgin olive oil

garlic

Wash the peppers, cut in half and remove the seeds and veins. Put them on an oiled baking tray and put in an oven preheated to 200°C/400°F/gas 6 for 10 minutes. Leave to cool.

Soak the breadcrumbs in the milk, then squeeze out the milk.

Remove the sausage meat from the casings. Mix the bread with the sausage meat, add the eggs and mix well.

Stuff the peppers with the mixture. Sprinkle over the 2 tablespoons of fresh breadcrumbs and drizzle extra virgin olive oil on top. Bake in an oven set at 200°C/400°F/gas 6 for 15 minutes.

Toast the bread on a griddle, then rub with a little garlic and drizzle olive oil on top. Serve the pepper halves on the crostini.

◆

Previous pages:
Fillet Steak Borbonica on Crostoni (page 126)
Bruschetta with Peppered Beef (page 110)

SALSICCE DI MAIALE MARCHIGIANO

PORK SAUSAGES

MAKES 18–20

1 kg/2¼ lb boneless pork shoulder, fat and lean
21 g/¾ oz [US 3½ teaspoons] salt
7 g/¼ oz [US 2 teaspoons] fresh coarsely ground black
pepper
2 cloves garlic, crushed
1 pinch grated nutmeg
1 pinch ground allspice
2 tablespoons dry white wine at room temperature
sausage casings (available from butchers)
wine at room temperature to soak casings

Mince [US grind] the pork and season with the salt, pepper, garlic and spices. Add the wine and mix together all the ingredients. Soak the casings in wine for 5 minutes, then using a sausage maker with a standard nozzle, make the sausages. Prick the sausages and hang them in a cool dry place for at least 3 days before using. These sausages will keep for up to 30 days hanging in the refrigerator.

CROSTINI DI FEGATO DI POLLO ALLA ARIELLA

CROSTINI OF CHICKEN LIVERS ARIELLA

We ate this recipe at La Diligenza, a lovely old coaching inn in the sleepy village of Borgopace not far from St Angelo in Vado, Marche. We had driven over a dramatic pass called the Bocca Trabaria. It was cold and a sharp wind was blowing off the snow-clad mountains as we descended into the village. The village air was pervaded with the odour of wood burning fires – we were in charcoal-makers' territory. Ariella, the chef/proprietor, with her husband Rodolpho, prepared these appetizing crostini for us.

SERVES 4

4 slices of bread for crostini
4 chicken livers
2 tablespoons finely chopped onion
2 tablespoons extra virgin olive oil
5 salted capers, well rinsed and dried
2 juniper berries, crushed
1 teaspoon finely chopped parsley
salt and freshly ground black pepper

Trim the livers and cut into small pieces. Fry the onion in the olive oil until browned, then add the livers, capers and crushed juniper berries and toss for 1 minute. Add the parsley and season with salt and freshly ground black pepper. Process the liver mixture to a paste. Toast the bread on a griddle. Top with the liver paste and serve.

———◆———

CROSTINI DI FEGATINI DI POLLO CON PARMIGIANO

CROSTINI OF CHICKEN LIVERS WITH PARMESAN

SERVES 4

8 slices of bread for crostini
150 g/5 oz chicken livers
1 tablespoon extra virgin olive oil
15 g/½ oz [US 1 tablespoon] butter
40 g/1½ oz fatty Parma ham, cut in julienne
½ medium onion, finely chopped
1 sprig fresh sage leaves, finely chopped
lemon juice
1 tablespoon freshly grated Parmesan cheese
salt and freshly ground black pepper

Clean the livers and chop into small pieces.
  Heat the oil and butter together in a frying pan and fry the ham and onion gently until the onion is golden. Add

the livers and the sage and fry briefly. Add a little lemon juice, the Parmesan cheese and salt and pepper to taste.

Toast the bread under a grill [US broiler]. Divide the liver mixture among the crostini. Serve at once.

CROSTINI CON PÂTÉ DI FEGATO DI POLLO

CROSTINI WITH CHICKEN LIVER PÂTÉ

This recipe is from Elizabeth David's book, *Mediterranean Food*. If you wish to keep this pâté for a few days, cover it with a film of melted butter.

SERVES 24

24 slices of bread for crostini
450 g/1 lb chicken livers
60 g/2 oz [US 4 tablespoons] butter
1 measure of dry sherry
2 measures of brandy
1 clove garlic, finely chopped and then mashed
1 pinch mixed spice [US apple pie spice]
1 pinch each dried thyme, basil and marjoram
salt and freshly ground black pepper
24 pickled cocktail gherkins

Clean the livers well, then sauté them in the butter for 3–4 minutes. The livers should still be pink inside. Remove the livers and reserve; add the sherry and brandy to the butter in the pan.

Mash or process the livers with the garlic, spice, herbs, salt and pepper, then add the juices from the pan. Keep in an earthenware terrine in the refrigerator until set.

Serve spread on hot crostini, which have been toasted on a griddle, with a cocktail gherkin fanned on top of each one.

CROSTINI DI FEGATINI AL VIN SANTO

CROSTINI OF CHICKEN LIVERS WITH VIN SANTO

SERVES 4

8 slices of bread for crostini

400 g / 14 oz chicken livers

200 ml / 7 fl oz [US ⅞ cup] extra virgin olive oil

1 red onion, finely chopped

170 ml / 6 fl oz [US ¾ cup] dry white wine

170 ml / 6 fl oz [US ¾ cup] vin santo

1 tablespoon salted capers, well rinsed and drained

4 anchovy fillets

salt and freshly ground black pepper

Heat the olive oil in a non-stick frying pan, add the onion and fry until pale golden. Add the chicken livers and fry, then add the dry white wine and vin santo and cook the livers until just done.

Put the chicken livers, cooking juices, capers and anchovies in a food processor and process, pulsing on and off, until finely chopped. Season with salt and freshly ground black pepper.

Toast the crostini on a griddle and spread with the chicken liver mixture. Serve at once.

◆

CROSTONI DI ROGNONE

CROSTONI OF VEAL KIDNEYS

SERVES 4

4 slices of bread for crostoni

4 veal kidneys

50 g / 1¾ oz [US 3½ tablespoons] butter

salt and freshly ground black pepper

170 ml / 6 fl oz [US ¾ cup] marsala

1 small can liver pâté, weighing approximately
85 g / 3 oz

Clean the kidneys and cut them into little bits. Heat the butter in a non-stick frying pan and gently cook the kidneys. Season them with salt and pepper. Remove the kidneys from the pan and keep them warm.

Add the marsala to the cooking juices and allow to reduce, then add the pâté, mixing in well.

Toast the bread under a grill [US broiler]. Serve the kidneys and the sauce on top of the crostoni. Serve at once.

CROSTONI CON ANIMELLE E FEGATINI

CROSTONI WITH SWEETBREADS AND CHICKEN LIVERS

SERVES 4

4 slices of bread for crostoni

2 sweetbreads, cleaned and chopped

3 chicken livers, cleaned and chopped

1 medium onion, very finely chopped

extra virgin olive oil

salt and freshly ground black pepper

1 tablespoon finely chopped parsley

red wine vinegar

Fry the onion gently in a little olive oil. Add the sweetbreads and gently fry for a few minutes, then add the livers and cook for a few more minutes. Season with salt, freshly ground black pepper, parsley and a splash of red wine vinegar.

Toast the bread on a griddle.

Spoon the sweetbread and liver mixture on top of the crostoni and serve at once.

Overleaf:
Skewers of Grilled Lamb on Bruschetta (page 112)
Crostini with Peppers and Sausage (page 102)

CROSTINI DI FEGATO DI MAIALE

CROSTINI OF PIG'S LIVER

SERVES 6

6 slices of bread for crostini

200 g / 7 oz pig's liver

1 clove garlic, finely chopped

4 anchovy fillets, chopped

2 hot chilli peppers preserved in vinegar, finely chopped

olive oil

1 pinch dried marjoram

salt and freshly ground black pepper

1 lemon

Chop the pig's liver very finely and add the garlic, anchovies and chilli peppers. Heat a little olive oil in a frying pan and add the liver mixture. Season with the marjoram, salt and freshly ground black pepper. Fry for a few minutes or until the liver is sealed, then add 2 tablespoons of water. Be careful not to overcook the liver.

Toast the bread on a griddle. Serve the liver mixture on the crostini and squeeze a little lemon juice over the top. Serve at once.

BRUSCHETTA CON PEPOSO

BRUSCHETTA WITH PEPPERED BEEF

A lot of pepper is needed for this dish so do not stint on the pepper.

Peposo was commonly prepared where there were terracotta kilns. A widely accepted story is that the workers who tended the brick kilns in the square during the construction of Brunelleschi's dome on the cathedral of Santa Maria del Fiore in Florence, which took 14 years to build and was finished in 1434, cooked peposo in the kilns for themselves and the rest of the workers.

Originally this recipe would have had 4 ingredients: the meat, pepper, red wine and garlic. Each of the flavouring ingredients had a purpose. The pepper was used to disguise the fact the meat would be in all probability starting to 'go off' due to there being no means of refrigeration. The wine was used so that the meat could be cooked for a long time without oil, and the garlic acted as a natural antibiotic in case of possible food poisoning! Salt was not added – poor people could not afford it. The tomato, which did not arrive in Europe until the 19th century was added to the recipe much later.

SERVES 4

4 slices of bread for bruschetta

800 g / 1¾ lb boneless shin of beef [US beef shank] plus the bone

2 cloves garlic

1 tablespoon tomato paste

salt

20 g / ¾ oz [US 2 tablespoons] freshly ground black pepper

robust red wine or water

Remove all the fat from the meat. Cut the meat into large cubes. Put the meat and the bone into a deep terracotta casserole with the garlic and tomato paste. Add some salt, the freshly ground black pepper and enough robust red wine or cold water to cover the meat.

Place a lid on the casserole and put it in an oven pre-heated to 160°C/300°F/gas 2. Cook very slowly for 4–5 hours. Add hot water if the sauce starts to dry out. Stir the meat mixture every now and then to make sure it is not sticking. When the cooking is completed, the sauce should be thick and rich.

Toast the bread on a griddle. Serve the meat and sauce on top of the bruschetta.

ROSTICINI SU BRUSCHETTA

SKEWERS OF GRILLED LAMB ON BRUSCHETTA

Rosticini are sold by street vendors everywhere in the Abruzzi region, especially on festival days, but only in the evening.

Olio Santo

All that is needed for *olio santo* is extra virgin olive oil and some fresh hot red chilli peppers. There are no hard and fast rules for this recipe. Slice some red chillies, about 12 for 340 ml / 12 fl oz of oil. Mix with oil and add a finely chopped clove of garlic if liked. Leave to marinate for a couple of days, and serve on rosticini.

SERVES 6

6 slices of bread for bruschetta

1 kg/2½ lb lamb, cut in 1.5 cm/½ in cubes

1 glass white wine

1 tablespoon extra virgin olive oil

juice of ½ lemon

salt and freshly ground black pepper

1 sprig fresh rosemary

30 wooden skewers soaked in water

Mix the wine, olive oil, lemon juice, salt and pepper together. Thread the lamb on the skewers.

Heat up a grill to very hot. A charcoal grill is preferable to an oven grill [US broiler]. Grill the lamb on the skewers (spiedini). When half cooked dip the sprig of rosemary in the wine mixture and brush the spiedini all over. Continue cooking.

Toast the bread on the charcoal grill or on a griddle. Serve the lamb on the bruschetta, with olio santo spooned over.

BRUSCHETTA CON COSTOLETTE DI MAIALE ALL'USO DI MONTEFELTRO

BRUSCHETTA WITH SPARE RIBS MONTEFELTRO

Il Montefeltro is a small territory which belonged to the dukedom of Urbino, the Montefeltro family. It is situated on the eastern edge of the Apennines, between the Conca stream and the river Marecchia. The main town of the area is San Leo, today famous for its hams and salamis. Montefeltro existed between the 13th century and the beginning of the 16th century. Pigmeat is from a pig which has been bred for bacon. The flavour of pig meat is very different to pork; it is much sweeter.

SERVES 6

6 slices of bread for bruschetta

500 g / 1¼ lb spare ribs

25 g / 1 oz [US 3 tablespoons] coarse sea salt

finely chopped garlic to taste

extra virgin olive oil

Put the spare ribs in an earthenware dish, (make sure they do not overlap). Sprinkle the sea salt all over the ribs, then leave to marinate for 2 days in a cool place. Turn the spare ribs after 1 day.

Wash the excess salt off the spare ribs and dry them thoroughly. Rub the spare ribs with garlic to taste.

Heat a grill [US broiler]. Place the ribs on a rack so that the fat can fall on to a tray underneath and grill. Toast the bread on a griddle. When the ribs are cooked serve them dribbled with extra virgin olive oil on the bruschetta.

◆

BRUSCHETTA CON RAGU DI SALSICCIA

BRUSCHETTA WITH SAUSAGE MEAT

SERVES 4

4 slices of bread for bruschetta

*300 g / 10 oz Marchigiani sausages (page 103), skinned,
or good pork sausage meat*

2 tablespoons extra virgin olive oil

50 g / 1¾ oz Parma ham

1 onion, finely chopped

8 plum tomatoes, peeled, seeded and cubed (concassé)

salt and freshly ground black pepper

Heat the extra virgin olive oil, add the Parma ham and
onion and fry until the onion is lightly golden. Add the
sausage meat and fry, breaking it up as it cooks. When
the sausage meat is cooked, add the concassé of tomatoes
and briefly cook until warmed through. If using the
home-made sausages, no seasoning is required; otherwise,
add some salt and pepper.

Toast the bread on a griddle. Spoon the sausage mixture
on top of each bruschetta and serve.

◆

BRUSCHETTA ALLA SALSICCIA DI FEGATO

BRUSCHETTA WITH LIVER SAUSAGE

A salad of rocket [US arugula] and chicory [US Belgian
endive], lightly dressed with olive oil and vinegar, goes
well with this bruschetta.

SERVES 4

4 slices of bread for bruschetta

4 pork and liver sausages (page 115)

2 tablespoons extra virgin olive oil

Remove the sausages from their skins. Heat the olive oil
in a frying pan and add the sausage meat, breaking it up

with a fork as you fry it. The final result should be a crumbly mixture.

Toast the bread on a griddle and divide the sausage meat and cooking juices among the bruschetta. Serve at once.

SALSICCE DI FEGATO

PORK AND LIVER SAUSAGES

MAKES APPROXIMATELY 32 SAUSAGES

1.4 kg/3 lb boneless pork shoulder

450g/1 lb pig's liver

grated zest of ¼ orange, blanched

60 g/2 oz [US 3½ tablespoons] salt

14 g/½ oz [US 4 teaspoons] fresh coarsely ground black pepper

2 cloves garlic, crushed

2 pinches grated nutmeg

2 pinches ground allspice

4 tablespoons dry white wine at room temperature

sausage casings (obtainable from butchers)

wine for soaking casings

Mince [US grind] the pork and liver. Add all the other ingredients and mix well. Soak the casings in wine for 5 minutes, then stuff with the mixture using a sausage maker with a standard nozzle.

Prick the sausages and hang in a cool dry place for 3 days before using them. These sausages have a 20-day life hanging in the refrigerator.

Fry the sausages in extra virgin olive oil or split them in half and cook them on a barbecue.

COLAZIONE DEL VIGNAROLO

THE VINEYARD WORKERS' BREAKFAST

For this you can use *cicoria catalana* instead of the
purple sprouting broccoli.

SERVES 4

4 slices of bread for bruschetta

200 g / 7 oz purple sprouting broccoli

150 g / 5 oz Italian sausage, skin removed

extra virgin olive oil

salt and freshly ground black pepper

2 cloves garlic, 1 of them finely chopped

dried hot chilli pepper flakes

3–4 tomatoes, peeled, seeded and cut into small cubes

2 tablespoons dry white wine

Boil the purple sprouting broccoli in salted water until it
is cooked. Drain thoroughly and toss in a little olive oil.
Season with salt and pepper. Keep warm.

Put a tablespoon of extra virgin olive oil in a frying pan
and add the finely chopped garlic and a good pinch of
dried chilli pepper flakes. Stir the garlic 2–3 times, then
add the sausage meat and fry for a few minutes. Add the
tomatoes and dry white wine. Simmer for 5 minutes over
a medium heat until the mixture has thickened.

In the meantime toast the bread on a griddle and rub
with the other clove of garlic cut in half.

Divide the purple sprouting broccoli among the
bruschetta and spoon the sausage and tomato mixture on
top. Serve immediately.

❖

Previous pages:
Crostini of Chicken Livers with Parmesan (page 104)
Crostini of Cotechino with Chutney (page 119)

CROSTINI DI COTECHINO CON CHUTNEY

CROSTINI OF COTECHINO WITH CHUTNEY

SERVES 3

12 slices of bread for crostini
1 cotechino (page 120), weighing 300 g/10 oz

Boil the cotechino. Toast the bread on a griddle. Slice the cotechino while still hot and place a slice on each crostini. Serve with a spoonful of tomato and onion chutney (see below) on top.

◆

POMODORO E CIPOLLA CHUTNEY

TOMATO AND ONION CHUTNEY

This chutney is not for storing. It is best used fresh and keeps for 3–4 days only.

100 g/3½ oz semi-ripe tomatoes
100 g/3½ oz small red onions
60 g/2 oz [US 5 tablespoons] sugar
2½ tablespoons red wine vinegar

Peel and seed the tomatoes and cut each into 8 sections. Peel the onions and cut each into 8 sections, then blanch. Caramelize the sugar with 1 tablespoon of the vinegar. Add the blanched onion and tomato. Toss the tomato and onion in the caramel, reduce the caramel by half, then add the remaining vinegar and reduce to a syrup.

◆

COTECHINO

MAKES 3 X 300 G / 10 OZ APPROX.

500 g/1 lb 2 oz boneless pork shoulder

200 g/7 oz pork belly [US fresh side pork]

300 g/10 oz pig skin

2 tablespoons salt

1 teaspoon mixed spices (see below)

¼ teaspoon saltpetre

1 clove garlic, crushed

*sausage casings; the finished result should be
3 cotechino 5cm/2in wide x 20cm/8in long (available
from butchers)*

white wine for soaking casings

For the mixed spices grind together:

1 tablespoon black peppercorns

3–4 cloves

1 x 4 cm/1½ in piece cinnamon

pinch of nutmeg

2 blades mace

2 dried bay leaves

pinch of dried thyme

Mince [US grind] the meats. Chop the skin finely. Mix together with the seasonings. Soak the casings in wine for 5 minutes, then stuff the mixture into the casings. A sausage maker is required for this operation.

Hang the cotechini in a dry, cool place and leave for 20 days at least before using. Don't allow the cotechini to touch each other.

To cook. Wrap the cotechino in a clean white napkin and tie it up. Place the cotechino in cold water and slowly bring it to the boil. Reduce the heat and boil gently. The time required is:

300 g/10 oz	1¾ hours
500 g/1 lb 2 oz	2 hours
1 kg/2½ lb	3 hours

FETTUNTA CON CANNELLINI E PANCETTA

FETTUNTA WITH CANNELLINI BEANS AND PANCETTA

Fettunta and bruschetta are interchangeable – they are exactly the same thing.

SERVES 4

4 slices of bread for bruschetta

300 g / 10 oz [US 1½ cups] cooked cannellini beans

115 g / 4 oz sliced pancetta, cut in julienne

extra virgin olive oil

3 cloves garlic, finely chopped

10 fresh sage leaves, finely chopped

salt and freshly ground black pepper

Heat 1 tablespoon of olive oil in a frying pan over a medium heat, add the pancetta and cook until crisp. Remove the bacon and drain on kitchen paper.

Heat 4 tablespoons of olive oil in the frying pan over medium heat, add the garlic and sage and stir until the garlic is pale gold. Add the beans and pancetta, season with salt and pepper and cook, stirring, for 3 minutes.

Toast the bread on a griddle. Spoon the beans on top and serve at once.

◆

BRUSCHETTA ALLO SPECK

BRUSCHETTA WITH SPECK

Speck is a type of prosciutto – salted and smoked lean and fat. It can be cooked or eaten raw.

SERVES 4

4 slices of bread for bruschetta

115 g / 4 oz sliced speck

½ onion, finely chopped

2 tablespoons extra virgin olive oil

1 clove garlic

100 g / 3½ oz Parmesan cheese in a piece
salt and freshly ground black pepper

Gently fry the onion in the extra virgin olive oil, over a
low heat. Season with salt and pepper. After 10 minutes,
add the speck cut in thin strips and fry for a minute or
two.

Toast the bread on a griddle and rub with the garlic cut
in half. Cover the bruschetta with the speck and onion
mixture and shave the Parmesan cheese on top. Serve at
once.

◆

BRUSCHETTA CON PANCETTA

BRUSCHETTA WITH PANCETTA

This goes very well with Fettunta con cannellini e
pancetta (page 121). Pancetta is the Italian form of
streaky bacon.

SERVES 4

4 slices of bread for bruschetta
24 slices of pancetta
2 cloves garlic, finely chopped
extra virgin olive oil

Toast the bread on a griddle. Rub the bread with the
garlic and sprinkle with extra virgin olive oil.

In the meantime cook the pancetta in a non-stick frying
pan. Put 6 slices of pancetta on each slice of bread. Serve
at once.

◆

TOURNEDOS ROSSINI

Gioacchino Rossini, the composer gourmet, equally well known as a prolific opera composer and lover of good food, came from Pesaro in the Marche. He was born in 1792 and died in 1868. The best known dish named after him is Tournedos Rossini. Rossini is said to have given the recipe to the chef at the Café Anglais in Paris.

SERVES 4

4 slices of bread for crostini (same size as the base of the steak)

4 fillet steaks [US filet mignons], weighing 200g/7 oz each

90 g/3 oz pâté de foie gras, cut in thin slices

1 black truffle, peeled

30 g/1 oz [US 2 tablespoons] butter

1 tablespoon olive oil

100 ml/3½ fl oz [US 7 tablespoons] Madeira or marsala

200 ml/7 fl oz [US ⅞ cup] stock

salt and freshly ground black pepper

Cut 4 slices from the truffle and chop the rest.

Heat the olive oil and butter in a frying pan. When foaming add the steaks. Cook over a strong heat until medium or rare, as preferred. Season with salt and freshly ground black pepper. Remove from the pan and keep warm.

Drain the butter and oil from the pan and deglaze with the Madeira or marsala. Add the stock and reduce by one-third, skimming off any impurities. Strain the sauce and add the chopped truffle.

While the sauce is reducing, fry the bread in butter. Put on each a slice of pâté de foie gras the same size as the crostini. Place under a hot grill [US broiler] for 2 minutes.

Place the steaks on top of the crostini. Put a slice of

FILETTO ALLA BORBONICA SU CROSTONI

FILLET STEAK BORBONICA ON CROSTONI

SERVES 4

4 slices of bread for crostoni
4 fillet steaks [US filet mignons], 150 g/6 oz each
extra virgin olive oil
salt
170 ml/6 fl oz [US ¾ cup] dry white wine
4 slices of mozzarella cheese
4 anchovy fillets
170 ml/6 fl oz [US ¾ cup] marsala

Fry the steaks in 2 tablespoons olive oil. Season with salt. Add the white wine and cook for 2 minutes. Place a slice of mozzarella on top of each steak, put an anchovy on top of the mozzarella and add the marsala. Cook until the mozzarella has melted.

Fry the slices of bread in olive oil.

Place a steak on top of each crostoni and pour the sauce, which should be well reduced, over the top. Serve at once.

◆

Previous pages:
Fettunta with Cannelini Beans and Pancetta (page 121)
Bruschetta with Pancetta (page 122)

PERNICE ARROSTO SU CROSTONI

ROAST PARTRIDGE SERVED ON CROSTONI

SERVES 4

4 slices of bread for crostoni

4 partridges

225 g/8 oz [US 1 cup] butter

8 slices unsmoked streaky bacon [US thick bacon slices]

livers from the birds plus 2 chicken livers

1 pinch dried thyme

1 pinch ground mace

salt and freshly ground black pepper

olive oil

1 measure brandy

170 ml/6 fl oz [US ¾ cup] chicken stock

lemon wedges

Place a piece of butter in the cavity of each bird and spread most of the remaining butter over the breasts and legs of the birds. Wrap the birds in the streaky bacon.

Place the birds breast-side up on a rack in a roasting pan and roast in an oven preheated to 220°C/425°F/gas 7 for 20 minutes. When the bacon starts to brown turn the birds over. Remove the bacon 5 minutes before the end of the cooking time, and only at this point salt the bird.

Sauté the livers in the remaining butter until pink and season with thyme, mace, salt and pepper. Mash the livers with a fork.

Fry the slices of bread in olive oil. Spread the liver mixture on the crostoni, and place the birds on top. Deglaze the roasting pan with a measure of brandy, flame, add the stock and reduce till slightly thickened. Strain the sauce and pour over the partridges. Serve the partridges with lemon wedges.

QUAGLIE SU CROSTINI CON UVA

QUAILS ON CROSTINI WITH GRAPES

SERVES 4

8 slices of bread for crostini

8 quails

200 g / 7 oz seedless green grapes

8 fresh sage leaves

8 small sprigs fresh rosemary

8 slices of pancetta or streaky bacon

salt and freshly ground black pepper

extra virgin olive oil

½ glass dry white wine

50 g / 1¾ oz [US 3½ tablespoons] butter

Put a sage leaf and sprig of rosemary inside each quail and wrap a slice of pancetta round each bird. Put the quails in a roasting pan, season with salt and pepper and pour a little extra virgin olive oil over each bird.

Roast the birds in an oven preheated to 200°C/400°F/ gas 6 for 15 minutes, adding the dry white wine half-way through the cooking. Baste the birds every now and then with the cooking juices. A few minutes before the end of cooking add the grapes to the roasting pan to warm through.

Fry the slices of bread in the butter. Place a quail on top of each slice. Serve the quails with the grapes and a little of the cooking juices.

◆

QUAGLIE ARROSTO CON SALVIA SU CROSTINI

ROAST QUAILS WITH SAGE ON CROSTINI

SERVES 4

8 slices of bread for crostini

8 plump quails

8 sprigs fresh sage

100 g/3½ oz [US 7 tablespoons] butter

8 slices streaky bacon [US thick bacon slices]

salt and freshly ground black pepper

olive oil

lemon wedges

Salt and pepper the quails. Stuff each one with a sprig of sage and put a little butter inside each cavity. Spread the rest of the butter on the breasts and legs of the birds. Wrap the streaky bacon around each bird, making sure the thighs of the bird are covered. Place the quails in a roasting pan and roast in an oven preheated to 200°C/400°F/gas 6 for 15 minutes.

Fry the bread in olive oil. Set a quail on each slice. Serve with lemon wedges.

———◆———

Overleaf:
Roast Partridge Served on Crostoni (page 127)
Roast Quails with Sage on Crostini (page 129)

ROAST WOODCOCK

Woodcock is a very prized species of game. It is a small bird and the dark flesh has a decidedly strong wild flavour. Allow the birds to hang for 3–4 days. Woodcock are not usually drawn and should be served medium to rare after 10–20 minutes cooking at the most.

SERVES 4

4 slices of bread for crostini

4 woodcock

115 g/4 oz butter, melted

8 rashers streaky bacon

salt and pepper

2 spirit measures brandy

Brush the woodcock with the melted butter. Wrap 2 rashers of streaky bacon around each bird. Roast the woodcock in an oven set at 200°C/400°F/gas 6, for 10–20 minutes (rare or medium).

Toast the bread and place under the birds 5 minutes into the cooking time to catch the trail as it drops out. Before the birds are cooked, remove the bacon, baste the birds and return to the oven to brown.

Remove the roasting pan from the oven, season the birds with salt and freshly ground black pepper. Place the pan on a high heat, pour over the warmed brandy and set it alight. Let the flames die out and serve at once. (A simple accompaniment of watercress and game chips is all that is necessary.)

CROSTINI DI CAPPERI (ARTUSI)

CROSTINI OF CAPERS

Pellegrino Artusi was the greatest Italian cookery writer of the 19th century. His book *La scienza in cucina e l'arte di mangiar bene* is still being printed. Artusi was born in Folimpopoli in Romagna, but lived in Florence and Viareggio.

SERVES 6

6 slices of bread for crostini

50 g/1¾ oz capers in vinegar

30 g/1 oz sultanas [US 3 tablespoons golden raisins]

20 g/¾ oz Parma ham in one slice

flour

50 g/1¾ oz icing sugar [US ⅓ cup confectioners' sugar]

2 teaspoons vinegar

20 g/¾ oz [US 3½ tablespoons] pine nuts

20 g/¾ oz [US 2 tablespoons] finely chopped candied fruit

light olive oil

Chop the capers roughly. Wash the sultanas and dry thoroughly. Cut the Parma ham into small cubes.

Put a bare tablespoon of flour in a saucepan with 2 tablespoons of the icing sugar. Place the pan over a moderate heat and stir the flour and sugar with a wooden spoon until the mixture is coloured brown. Add 6 tablespoons of water with the vinegar and bring to the boil, beating the mixture well until softened again. Add the rest of the ingredients and cook for 10 minutes, stirring constantly. Taste and add more vinegar if necessary – this mixture should have a sweet and sour taste. It is impossible to give the exact quantity of vinegar as vinegars vary in strength.

Fry the crostini in light olive oil or toast them lightly on a griddle. Pour the mixture on top of the crostini and serve at once.

BRUSCHETTA MADE WITH POLENTA AND FLAT BREADS

PIADINA CON ZUCCHINI ALLA GRIGLIA E FORMAGGIO DI CAPRA

PIADINA WITH GRIDDLED ZUCCHINI AND GOAT'S CHEESE

La piadina, the typical focaccia romagnola – also called piada or pie – originally was usually eaten with *squaqueron,* a soft local cheese, or with salami, prosciutto or sausage. In more recent years a whole new lot of ideas for piada toppings has evolved. The following is one of them.

SERVES 4

4 freshly made piadina (page 21)

250 g/8 oz (12 slices) zucchini, cut lengthways

two 100 g/3½ oz fresh goat's cheeses

4 tablespoons extra virgin olive oil

1 tablespoon chopped fresh mint

1 tablespoon chopped parsley

1 clove garlic, finely chopped

1 pinch dried hot chilli flakes

salt and freshly ground black pepper

Heat a griddle and cook the zucchini on both sides. Put the zucchini in a shallow dish and dress with the oil, mint, parsley, garlic, chilli flakes, salt and freshly ground black pepper.

With a knife dipped in hot water, cut the goat's cheeses in half, making four discs. Heat the goat's cheeses through in the oven or put under a grill [US broiler] for a few minutes.

On one half of each piadina, assemble 3 slices of zucchini slightly folded. Dribble some of the oil and herb dressing over the slices of zucchini. Place the warmed goat's cheese on the other half, sprinkle some freshly ground black pepper on the goat's cheese and serve at once.

Previous pages:
Piadina with Zucchini and Parmesan (page 140)
Piadina with Radicchio and Pancetta (page 137)

PIADINA CON MOZZARELLA E PROSCIUTTO

PIADINA WITH MOZZARELLA AND PROSCIUTTO

SERVES 4

4 freshly made piadina (page 21)
2 mozzarella, preferably bufala weighing
approximately 125 g/4½ oz each
8 slices of Parma ham

Slice and divide the mozzarella among the piadina. Place under a hot grill [US broiler]. As soon as the mozzarella is softened, put 2 slices of Parma ham on top of each piadina and serve at once.

◆

PIADINA CON RADICCHIO E PANCETTA

PIADINA WITH RADICCHIO AND PANCETTA

SERVES 4

4 freshly made piadina (page 21)
2 small radicchio di Treviso
8 slices of Pancetta
1 clove garlic, finely chopped
1 tablespoon finely chopped parsley
extra virgin olive oil
salt and freshly ground black pepper

Prepare a sauce with the garlic, parsley, 3 tablespoons extra virgin olive oil, salt and pepper.

Wash and thoroughly dry the radicchio and cut each lengthways into four. Sprinkle the radicchio with a little oil and grill under a hot grill [US broiler], turning the pieces over. Grill the pancetta until crispy.

Put two quarters of radicchio and 2 slices of pancetta on each piadina and spoon a little of the parsley and garlic sauce on top. Serve at once.

RADICCHIO TREVISANO ALLA GRIGLIA CON MOZZARELLA E TARTUFI CON PIADINA

PIADINA WITH GRILLED RADICCHIO, MOZZARELLA AND TRUFFLES

SERVES 4

4 freshly made piadina (page 21)

4 small or 2 large heads of radicchio di Treviso

*2 fresh mozzarella di bufala, weighing approximately
125 g/4½ oz each, cut in slivers*

3 tablespoons extra virgin olive oil

salt and freshly ground black pepper

115 g/4 oz Parmesan cheese, cut in slivers

2 white truffles, shaved

Remove any damaged leaves from the radicchio heads, cut each lengthways in half or quarters, depending on the size, and wash thoroughly. Leave to drain in a colander.

Put the radicchio on a plate and put slivers of mozzarella between the leaves. Dribble the olive oil over the top and season well with salt and freshly ground black pepper.

Heat a large frying pan over a high heat and, when hot, add the radicchio pieces in one layer. Cook for only 3 minutes, turning very carefully once. Arrange the Parmesan slivers on top of the radicchio and flash under a hot grill [US broiler] until the cheese has melted. Top with the shaved truffle and place on top of the piadina. Serve at once.

◆

PIADINA CON STRACCHINO E RUCOLA

PIADINA WITH STRACCHINO AND ROCKET

Stracchino is a soft cow's milk cheese similar to the more commonly known taleggio.

SERVES 4

4 freshly made piadina (page 21)
120 g/4 oz stracchino cheese
2 handfuls of rocket [US arugula]
salt

Dot one-quarter of the stracchino over each warm piadina. Put in a preheated moderate oven for a few minutes until the stracchino is warmed through slightly.

Sprinkle the rocket very lightly with salt and toss. Place a small bunch in the middle of each piadina. Serve at once. The piadina can be folded over to eat.

◆

PIADINA AL GORGONZOLA E PROSCIUTTO COTTO

PIADINA WITH GORGONZOLA AND COOKED HAM

Taleggio can be used instead of gorgonzola.

SERVES 4

4 freshly made piadina (page 21)
200 g/7 oz sweet gorgonzola cheese
4 large slices of cooked ham
fresh basil

Heat a grill [US broiler].

Distribute small pieces of gorgonzola all over the piadina. Place the piadina under the grill and leave until the cheese has melted. While the piadina are still hot put the ham on top and garnish with a few basil leaves. Serve at once.

PIADINA CON ZUCCHINE E PARMIGIANO

PIADINA WITH ZUCCHINI AND PARMESAN

SERVES 4

4 freshly made piadina (page 21)
400 g / 14 oz zucchini sliced lengthways
4 anchovy fillets, mashed
2 tablespoons finely chopped parsley
3 tablespoon extra virgin olive oil
juice of ½ lemon
freshly ground black pepper
parmesan cheese

Sprinkle the zucchini with salt and leave to drain in a colander for half an hour. Dry the zucchini with a cloth.

Cook the zucchini on a griddle and immediately dress with a sauce made of the mashed anchovies with parsley, extra virgin olive oil, lemon juice and freshly ground black pepper. Leave the zucchini to marinate for half an hour.

Serve on warm piadina with shavings of Parmesan on top.

◆

PIADINA CON NOCI E FORMAGGIO DI CAPRA

PIADINA WITH WALNUTS AND GOAT'S CHEESE

SERVES 4

4 freshly made piadina (page 21)
40 g / 1½ oz walnut halves
200 g / 7 oz mature firm goat's cheese
200 g / 7 oz mixed small salad leaves
85 g / 3 oz celery, cut in matchsticks
2 plum tomatoes, peeled and diced
2 tablespoons red wine vinegar
5 tablespoons extra virgin olive oil
salt and freshly ground black pepper

Toss the salad leaves, celery and tomatoes in a dressing made by whisking the vinegar, oil, 2 pinches of salt and a generous pinch of pepper together with a fork.

Divide the salad leaves, celery and tomatoes among the warm piadina. Scatter the walnuts over and shave the cheese on top. Serve at once.

◆

PIADINA CON SPINACI

PIADINA WITH SPICED SPINACH

SERVES 4–6

4 freshly made piadina (page 21)

900 g / 2 lb fresh spinach, trimmed

3 tablespoons extra virgin olive oil

½ onion, finely chopped

2 cloves garlic, finely chopped

1 pinch ground cinnamon

1 pinch freshly grated nutmeg

5 tablespoons pine nuts, toasted

2 tablespoons small seedless raisins

115 g / 4 oz fresh ricotta cheese

salt and freshly ground black pepper

115 g / 4 oz Parmesan cheese, freshly grated

Cook the spinach with a little salt and with only the water left on the leaves after washing them. Leave them to drain thoroughly in a sieve. Chop the spinach coarsely.

Heat the olive oil in a frying pan over medium heat and fry the onion and garlic until soft and pale golden. Add the spinach, spices, pine nuts and raisins and stir until the spinach is reheated. Add the ricotta and stir in. Season with salt and pepper. Add the Parmesan and toss into the mixture.

Serve on hot piadina and eat at once.

PIADINA CON FUNGHI E RUCOLA

PIADINA WITH MUSHROOMS AND ROCKET

SERVES 4

4 freshly made piadina (page 21)
60 g / 2 oz Gruyère cheese
200 g / 7 oz button mushrooms, sliced
6 tablespoons extra virgin olive oil
2 tablespoons lemon juice
salt and freshly ground black pepper
1 handful of rocket [US arugula]
100 g / 4 oz young spinach leaves

Heat a grill [US broiler].

Grate the Gruyère and scatter over the piadina. Place the piadina under the grill and leave until the Gruyère has melted.

Meanwhile, quickly fry the mushrooms in 2 tablespoons of extra virgin olive oil. Season with salt and freshly ground black pepper. Divide the mushrooms among the piadina.

Whisk together the lemon juice, remaining extra virgin olive oil and a little salt and pepper. Use to dress the rocket and spinach and place the leaves in the centre of the piadina. Serve at once.

◆

PIADINA AL TONNO

PIADINA WITH TUNA

SERVES 4

4 freshly made piadina (page 21)
1 can tuna in olive oil
4 tomatoes, peeled, seeded and cubed

Previous pages:
Polenta Crostini with Mushrooms (page 149)
Polenta Bruschetta with Taleggio and Mushrooms (page 145)

4 tablespoons extra virgin olive oil
8 fresh basil leaves
1 tablespoon finely chopped parsley
salt and freshly ground black pepper
50 g / 1¼ oz black olives, pitted
50 g / 1¼ oz green olives, pitted
1 small red onion, finely sliced

Toss the tomatoes in the olive oil with the torn basil, chopped parsley and some salt and pepper.

Scatter the tomatoes over the warm piadina. Break up the tuna and scatter over the tomatoes. Finish by scattering over the olives and onion. Serve at once.

◆

POLENTA CON TALEGGIO E FUNGHI

POLENTA BRUSCHETTA WITH TALEGGIO AND MUSHROOMS

For toasting polenta bruschetta, the griddle should be
red hot and dry.

SERVES 4

4 slices of cold polenta (page 22) for bruschetta
150 g / 5 oz taleggio cheese, cut in small cubes
400 g / 14 oz fresh porcini (ceps) or shiitake mushrooms
2 tablespoons extra virgin olive oil
1 clove garlic, finely chopped
1 tablespoon finely chopped parsley
salt and freshly ground black pepper

Slice the mushrooms and fry in the olive oil until cooked but still firm. Add the garlic and parsley and season with salt and freshly ground black pepper.

Toast the polenta on a griddle for 3–4 minutes per side. Put the mushrooms on top of the polenta and sprinkle the taleggio on top of the hot mushrooms; the cheese will melt slightly. Serve at once.

BRUSCHETTA DI POLENTA CON UOVA STRAPAZZATE E FUNGHI PORCINI

POLENTA BRUSCHETTA WITH SCRAMBLED EGG AND
PORCINI MUSHROOMS

SERVES 4

4 slices of cold polenta (page 22) for bruschetta

450 g/1 lb fresh porcini (ceps) or shiitake mushrooms

8 eggs

145 g/5 oz [US 10 tablespoons] butter

salt and freshly ground black pepper

4 tablespoons milk

balsamic vinegar

Toast the polenta on a red hot, dry griddle; keep warm. Slice the mushrooms and fry them in 30 g/1 oz [US 2 tablespoons] of the butter; keep warm.

Crack the eggs into a bowl. Season with salt and freshly ground black pepper, add the milk and beat together. Add the remaining butter in small bits. Scramble the eggs in a non-stick pan.

Amalgamate the porcini with the scrambled eggs. Spoon the mixture over the polenta bruschetta. Sprinkle a little balsamic vinegar over the scrambled egg. Serve at once.

◆

BRUSCHETTA DI POLENTA E BACCALA

POLENTA BRUSCHETTA WITH SALT COD

SERVES 6

6 slices of cold polenta (page 22) for bruschetta

300 g/10 oz salt cod

6 anchovy fillets

1 clove garlic, finely chopped

90 ml/3 fl oz [US 6 tablespoons] extra virgin olive oil

2 tablespoons white wine vinegar

2 tablespoons finely chopped parsley

Soak the salt cod for 2 days, changing the water regularly.

Cook the fish in plenty of boiling water for about 20 minutes or until soft; drain. Remove the skin and bones and flake the fish into a bowl.

Mash the anchovy fillets with a fork. Add the garlic and mash into the anchovy paste. Mix the oil and vinegar together. Add the parsley and the anchovy mixture and stir in well. Pour the sauce over the fish. Leave to marinate for about 15 minutes, covered, in a warm place.

Toast the polenta on a red hot, dry griddle. Serve the salt cod spooned on top of the polenta slices.

------◆------

CROSTINI DI POLENTA CON FUNGHI AL POMODORO

POLENTA CROSTINI WITH MUSHROOMS AND TOMATO

Serves 4

4 slices of cold polenta (page 22) for crostini

350 g/12 oz fresh porcini (ceps), shiitake or mixed wild mushrooms

2 tomatoes, peeled, seeded and diced

200 ml/7 fl oz [US ⅞ cup] extra virgin olive oil

3 cloves garlic, finely chopped

2 springs of fresh mint, finely chopped

dry white wine

salt and freshly ground black pepper

olive oil for frying polenta

Slice the mushrooms and fry them in the extra virgin olive oil, adding the garlic and mint. Add the tomatoes and fry for a few seconds. Add a splash of dry white wine and briskly reduce. Season with salt and freshly ground black pepper.

Fry the polenta in olive oil until crispy. Serve the mushroom and tomato mixture on top of the fried polenta.

IL PEPOSO DELL'IMPRUNETA CON BRUSCHETTA DI POLENTA

PEPOSO OF IMPRUNETA WITH POLENTA BRUSCHETTA

This is a more sophisticated recipe for peposo. It is based on a recipe of Giuseppe Alessi. He remarks that originally peposo was eaten by the brickmakers after a long hard night's work in Impruneta, which is a town near Florence once noted for its kilns. There are still potters carrying on traditional pot-making in Impruneta.

SERVES 4

4 slices of cold polenta (page 22) for bruschetta

600 g / 1 lb 5 oz beef shin, [US beef shank meat]
cut in cubes

2 stalks celery

1 carrot

1 medium onion

1 clove garlic

10 tablespoons olive oil

1 sprig of rosemary tied securely
together with string

2 bay leaves tied securely
together with string

1 strip of lemon zest tied securely
together with string

4 sprigs of parsley tied securely
together with string

750 ml / 1¼ pt [US 3 cups] water

250 ml / 8 fl oz [US 1 cup] robust red wine

1 good pinch dried oregano

1 good pinch dried marjoram

1 good pinch dried basil

1 clove

1 pinch mixed spice [US apple pie spice]

3 black peppercorns

salt and coarsely ground black pepper

Gremolata
grated zest of 1 orange
grated zest of 1 lemon

Roughly chop the vegetables. Heat the oil in a terracotta or cast iron casserole and add the roughly chopped vegetables and the bouquet of herbs and peel. Cook the vegetables until they are wilted. Add the meat. Leave to cook, but do not allow the meat to brown.

In a saucepan, bring the water, wine, herbs and spices to the boil. Lower the heat and simmer for 5 minutes.

Add the wine and water mixture to the meat and vegetables and mix together well. Season with salt. Cover the casserole and place in an oven preheated to 160°C/ 300°F/gas 2. Leave to cook for 4–5 hours.

Before serving remove the bunch of herbs and, if possible, the clove! Spoon on to slices of polenta toasted on a red hot, dry griddle. Sprinkle with the gremolata and a generous sprinkling of coarsely ground black pepper. Serve at once.

CROSTINI DI POLENTA CON FUNGHI IN BIANCO

POLENTA CROSTINI WITH MUSHROOMS

SERVES 4

4 slices of cold polenta (page 22) for crostini
350 g/12 oz fresh porcini (ceps), shiitake or mixed wild mushrooms
200 ml/7 fl oz [US ⅞ cup] virgin olive oil
3 cloves garlic, finely chopped
2 sprigs of fresh mint, finely chopped
dry white wine
salt and freshly ground black pepper

Slice the mushrooms and fry them in the olive oil, adding the garlic and the mint. Add a splash of dry white wine, briskly reduce and season with salt and freshly ground black pepper.

BRUSCHETTA DI POLENTA ALLA CARNICA

POLENTA BRUSCHETTA WITH PORCINI AND PANCETTA

This recipe is from the Friuli area.

SERVES 4

4 slices of cold polenta (page 22) for bruschetta

150 g / 5 oz fresh porcini (ceps), sliced

12 slices of pancetta

4 slices of fresh Montasio cheese or Asiago

30 g / 1 oz [US 2 tablespoons] butter

Toast the polenta on a red hot, dry griddle.

First, place a slice of cheese and then 3 slices of pancetta on each slice of polenta. Put the polenta slices in a preheated hot oven to gratinate.

Fry the sliced mushrooms in the butter and divide among the polenta bruschetta. Serve at once.

◆

CROSTONI DI POLENTA CON LE UOVA E FUNGHI

CROSTONI OF POLENTA WITH EGG AND MUSHROOMS

SERVES 4

4 slices of cold polenta (page 22) for crostoni

4 eggs

300 g / 10 oz cultivated mushrooms

70 g / 2½ oz [US 5 tablespoons] butter

1 clove garlic, finely chopped

2 tablespoons finely chopped parsley

salt and freshly ground white pepper

Slice the mushrooms. Heat 50 g/1¾ oz [US 3½ tablespoons] of the butter in a non-stick frying pan and add

Previous pages:
Crescente with Fried Artichokes and Parmesan (page 154)

the mushrooms and garlic. Sauté the mushrooms, then add the parsley and season with salt.

In the remaining butter gently fry the eggs. Season with salt and freshly ground white pepper.

As the eggs are frying, toast the polenta on a red hot, dry griddle.

Divide the mushrooms among the polenta crostoni and place an egg on top. Serve at once.

CRESCENTE CON PROSCIUTTO DI PARMA

CRESCENTE WITH PARMA HAM

For this very simple but appetizing dish all that is needed is a beautiful slice of Parma ham gently dropped on to a hot crescente (page 20) and eaten at once.

CRESCENTE CON SCAGLIE DI FORMAGGIO

CRESCENTE WITH PARMESAN SHAVINGS

Cook the crescente as indicated in the recipe on page 20 and serve with Parmesan shavings on top.

CRESCENTE CON BRESAOLA E RUCOLA

CRESCENTE WITH BRESAOLA AND ROCKET

SERVES 4

4 freshly made crescente (page 20)
bresaola
8 pickled gherkins
2 handfuls of rocket [US arugula]
extra virgin olive oil
vinegar

Put some slices of bresaola on the hot crescente (use a light hand so that the bresaola does not fall flat). Slice the gherkins and scatter over. Place a small mound of rocket, lightly dressed with extra virgin olive oil and vinegar, in the centre. Do not use salt; the bresaola is salty enough. Serve at once, while the crescente is still hot.

◆

CRESCENTE CON CARCIOFI E POMODORI SECCHI

CRESCENTE WITH ROASTED ARTICHOKE AND DRIED TOMATO

SERVES 4

4 freshly made crescente (page 20)

4 roasted artichokes preserved in sunflower oil (available from delicatessens), drained

4 sun-dried tomato halves preserved in oil, drained

Parmesan cheese

coarse sea salt

Season the crescente lightly with sea salt.

Slice the artichokes and divide them among the crescente. Cut each tomato half into 10 strips. Scatter the dried tomatoes over the artichokes, then shave Parmesan on the top. Serve at once.

◆

CRESCENTE CON CARCIOFI FRITTI E GRANA

CRESCENTE WITH FRIED ARTICHOKES AND PARMESAN

SERVES 4

4 freshly made crescente (page 20)

8 roasted artichockes preserved in sunflower oil (available from delicatessens), drained

Parmesan cheese

oil for frying

coarse sea salt

Season the crescente lightly with sea salt.

Slice the roasted artichokes and fry in plenty of oil until golden and crisp. Scatter the fried artichoke over the crescente and shave a good scattering of Parmesan on top. Serve at once.

◆

CRESCENTE AI POMODORI

CRESCENTE WITH TOMATOES

SERVES 4

4 freshly made crescente (page 20)

3 large plum tomatoes

salt

1 tablespoon extra virgin olive oil

6 fresh basil leaves, roughly chopped

6 fresh mint leaves, roughly chopped

◆

Peel and seed the tomatoes and cut them into small cubes. Sprinkle a pinch of salt and the olive oil over the tomatoes. Toss the tomatoes with the herbs and leave to marinate for 10 minutes.

Scatter the tomatoes over the hot crescente and eat at once.

◆

RECIPE INDEX

◆